Mindset Shift
– Unlocking Your Path to Success

DrStem Sithembile Mahlatini

No One Can Get in The Way of a Made-up Mind.

Drstem Sithembile Mahlatini

You are Worthy, Able and Capable

I wanted to become famous to prove I was a worthy person, but eventually I realized only you can make yourself feel worth. **Davina McCall**

Acknowledgement

Star Sithabile Mahlatini-Kahari
Star Salon Suites Peabody, Mass USA
(Coming World Wide)
https://www.starksalonsuites.com/

I salute you Boss Lady. You are Leading The way. So proud and happy to say, you are my sister and role model. Thank you.

DrStem Sithembile Mahlatini *is a Selflove, Self-confidence Coach, workshop Facilitator and Speaker who specializes in Personal and Leadership Coaching. She is the President and Founder of The DrStem Empowerment Conference, The Annual Bounce Back Empowerment Conference, The Bounce Back Empowerment Seminars and Workshops as well as The Bounce Back Book Series . She is originally from Zimbabwe. She currently resides in Orlando, FL USA.*

Visit DrStem online at www.drstemmie.com or email her at drstem14@gmail.com

Be You Be Free
Become Unstoppable
You are Unique and Complete

When your life looks like a mountain, impossible to climb, don't ever forget how incredible you are. Whatever, dream, desire or passion you have, remember, mindset shift will help you see all the resources that are already within and around you.

The impression you convey is an expression of yourself that depends upon your innermost thoughts and feelings. Do not be afraid. When you walk in your confident shoes your bright spirit will always attract success.

Your originality and special flair make you unique, fabulous, glorious, and amazing, so love the skin you are in unconditionally, and know your true worth, every single day.

Each time you strive to be your highest self, you are an inspiration to all those around you, let your light shine unapologetically.

Your inner conviction and love for life will see you through difficult times and even in your darkest moments this light within will sustain you.

Mindset Shift opens up self-belief. Self-belief gives you the will to reach for your best and succeed at whatever your heart desires, no matter what the circumstances are. The past has no power over you, with mindset shift, you can make new confident choices in the present moment-now. **Yes You Can.**

The Mindset Shift – Unlocking Your Path to Ultimate Success. Copyright © 2024 by Dr. Stem Sithembile Mahlatini

www.drstemmie.com

All rights reserved. No part of this publication may be reproduced, distributed, or transmitted in any form or by any means, including photocopying, recording, or other electronic or mechanical methods, without the prior written permission of the author, except in the case of brief quotations embodied in reviews and certain other non-commercial uses permitted by copyright law. Excluded from this copyright are the contributing authors who maintain all rights to the material inside the chapter he or she wrote for this book.

Disclaimer—The advice, guidelines, and all suggested material in this book is given in the spirit of information with no claims to any particular guaranteed outcomes. This book does not replace professional consultation. Anyone deciding to add physical or mental exercises to their life should reach out to a licensed medical doctor or therapist before following any of the advice in this book. The author, publisher, editor, and organizer do not assume and hereby disclaim any liability to any party for any loss, damage, or disruption caused by anything written in this book.

ISBN:	979-8-9864291-3-7
Cover Design:	Faizan Siddiqui
Interior Design:	Faizan Siddiqui
Publisher:	DrStem Global Training Coaching & Consulting Services, Inc. Orlando

Acknowledgements

Dad Benjamin Mahlatini

Much love and appreciation to the two people that gave birth to this beautiful soul "Me", my dad Benjamin Mahlatini and Mom Idah Mahlatini.

I love both of you and thank you for your DNA, your prayers and unconditional love for me and all my siblings. Thank you for being The Best Parents Ever. I am the leader and trail blazer that I am because of your example, guidance and mentorship. I am blessed to be your first born.

Mom Idah Sanganza Mahlatini

To all my brothers, sisters and friends, you are too many to list, I love and appreciate you. Thank you for you unconditional love and support throughout the years. A big part of who I am is because of you.

To my Lord and Savior, I am glad I believed in you and continue to hold onto the hem of your gown. Thank you for creating and loving me unconditionally. It is all making sense. I believe in you, I believe in me.

I am so excited to see the rest of what you want me to do. I asked to be more than an ordinary servant and you answered.

Here is to Soaring, Inspiring, Encouraging and Empowering others.

Foreword

As of this publication, I do not have to walk on eggshells anymore. I can be myself. I believe om me. I trust myself. I trust life. I can make my own decisions and my own choices. I do not need to make anyone's opinion of me or of my choices determine who I become. I am free. There are no limits; the sky is not even a limit, and I can be who I want to be and do anything I want to do in divine order. There are no limitations to my happiness, my joy, my blessings, my possibilities, or my life. Zero limits. The saying "Be You, Be Free Become Unstoppable" is a true definition of who I now am. I am truly Unstoppable Free and Fearless.

This is my hope and prayer for you, the reader, that you too can Be You, Free, Fearless and Unstoppable.

Having a mindset shift has truly opened and unlocked many paths to success for me. I am delivered from the power of fear, lack, or anxiety. No weapon formed against me shall prosper. Doors of abundance, prosperity, eternal happiness, business, family, and success are now open to me. The Lord has not given me a spirit of fear, but of power and of love and of a sound mind.

I now love myself unconditionally. I give myself love. I open myself to the possibilities of life. It is so sweet to trust in Jesus, just to take him at his word.

Abraham Lincoln said, "All that I am and all I ever hope to be, I owe to my mother." I say, "All that I am and all I ever hope to be, I owe to my father and mother, Benjamin and Idah Mahlatini, whom I continue to give praises for being the best parents ever. Their love and guidance have made me all that I am and enabled all that I ever hoped to be. Because of them, I learned to lead, to dream, to live big, and to believe that all dreams come true.

I now know what Les Brown was talking about when he said, "Someone's opinion of you does not have to become your reality. ... Regardless of your circumstances you can succeed. Regardless of where you were born, who your parents are, your demographic area or your economical background you can succeed."

My hope is to instill this same message to you, the reader, and to all people that I will encounter in this lifetime. Yes I hope you attend The Bounce Back Empowerment Conference one day or join me in The Bounce Back Anthology Series as a Co-Author. More information on my website *www.drstemmie.com*

It is time to let your own light shine. I hope The Mindset Shift guides you to your greatness. Remember YOHO, You Only Have One Life. (If you have not viewed my Ted Talk on YouTube with same time YOHO, you can view it on *https://www.youtube.com/watch?v=I4GcbEGJW-c*

You Only Have One Life: Live it or Lose it | Dr. Stem Sithembile Mahlatini | TEDxCaledon
931 views 9mo ago ...more

 TEDx Talks 40.3M

Much Success To You.

Contents

Foreword 16

Introduction 18

Happiness: Cause or Effect? 21

The Truth about Money and Happiness 23

A Genuine Sense of Security 25

The Quest for Empowerment 27

Dissolving Emotional Blockages 28

Releasing the Past to Make Room for Something Better 30

Transforming Limiting Beliefs into Empowering Beliefs 32

The Keys to Happiness 35

Learning How to Love Yourself 37

Overcoming Negative Preconceptions 39

Getting to Know Yourself 41

Falling in Love with Your Uniqueness 44

Creating Meaningful Work 46

Doing What You Love for a Living 48

Identifying and Nurturing Your Talents 50

Learning How to Work Smart – Not Just Hard! 53

Making Time for What Really Matters 54

Show Me the Money 56

Developing a True Success Mind-Set 59

Developing A Belief in Yourself 60

Taking Responsibility for Where You Are Now 62

Making the Right Choices, Moment to Moment 65

Clear Out the Cobwebs and Make a Fresh Start 69

Allowing Yourself to Be Successful 72

What Does Attitude Have to Do with Success? 75

There is No Try, Only Do 77

The Joys and Evils of Expectations 80

Building Your Success Muscles with Discipline 83

Sacrifices: Making Room for What You Want 86

Conquering the Fear of Success 89

Goal-Setting, Simplified 92

Taking Action: Like a Match to Tinder 96

How to End Procrastination? 97

Making Your Action Steps Focused 99

Staying Motivated 100

Remember Your Dream 101

Reinforce the Benefits 102

See Obstacles as Mere Detours 103

Affirm the Possibilities 104

Avoid Burnout 106

Enjoying the Journey 107

Develop a True Attitude of Gratitude 108

Express Appreciation for Everything 109

It's All Up to You 111

The Deepest Desire of Your Heart by Will Edwards 112

Bonus Affirmations 113

Foreword

All these 59 years, here is what I have learned and come back to: It's all about choosing to believe in You.

Choosing to believe in yourself is a transformative decision that can shape the course of your life in profound ways. When you make the conscious choice to trust in your abilities, worth, and potential, you unlock a powerful force that can drive you towards success, fulfillment, and happiness.

Believing in you, trusting yourself is the foundation upon which all achievements are built. It is the unwavering confidence that propels you to take risks, pursue your dreams, and overcome obstacles. Without this belief, self-doubt can creep in, holding you back from reaching your full potential and living the life you desire. What a dream killer it is to doubt yourself and wait on others' approval.

When you choose to believe in yourself, you are choosing to embrace your strengths and acknowledge your worth. This self-assurance allows you to set ambitious goals, push past limitations, and persevere in the face of challenges. It empowers you to take ownership of your life and make decisions that align with your values and aspirations.

Believing in yourself also influences how others perceive you. Confidence is magnetic and inspires trust and respect from those around you. When you exude self-belief, you attract opportunities, forge meaningful relationships, and influence positive change in both your personal and professional spheres.

Moreover, choosing to believe in yourself is an act of self-love and self-care. It involves treating yourself with kindness, compassion, and encouragement, even in moments of failure or setback. By nurturing a positive self-image and cultivating self-confidence, you cultivate resilience and inner strength that can sustain you through life's ups and downs.

What a life. What awesome lessons I have learned.

I am telling you, the power of choosing to believe in yourself cannot be overstated. It is a decision that can lead to personal growth, professional success, and overall well-being.

So, to you my beloved reader, I say, embrace your potential, trust in your abilities, and have faith in your journey.

Remember that you are capable, worthy, and deserving of all the amazing things life has to offer.

Choose to believe in yourself, and watch as your life transforms in extraordinary ways.

Yes You Can and Yes You Will.

Say it with me:

Yes I Can and Yes I will.

Introduction

Most of us have an idea about what success means to us, and we have a mental vision of what it will look like when it arrives in our lives. We might finally get the career or business recognition we've been working so hard for, earn a lot of money, find the man or woman of our dreams, start a family, purchase our own home, buy the sports car we've wanted since we were a teenager, or reach any number of other personal accomplishments. Is this success? For some of us, it might be. Perhaps you have a different vision of what success means to you.

Regardless of your personal definition of success, you likely have one thing in common with the rest of us: you are still seeking the level of success you want to attain. Maybe you've had success in certain areas, but not in others. Your career might be going great, but your relationships are lacking. Or you've met the love of your life, but you just can't seem to earn the amount of money that would make you happy. Or everything else is great but you can't seem to lose those last 20 pounds and get into better shape.

It's a maddening position to be in, especially if you don't understand why it's happening. You may think you're doing everything right, but circumstances just won't bend to your will. You constantly run into obstacles, sabotage your own efforts, berate yourself for your "failures,"- and the struggle continues.

This struggle continues because of one reason, and one reason only: you are focusing your energy and effort in the wrong direction!

In this modern age, we have the misguided notion that success is some elusive quality "out there" that we need to hunt down and capture. We believe that if we say the right things, do the right things, take exactly the right steps, success will fly right into our little butterfly net and we can pin it down on a sheet of cardboard and hang it proudly on our wall.

We can't capture success, nor can we buy it, stumble across it, or fall into it. We can only create it, from the inside out. And the only way to create it is by changing our thoughts and habits.

What do thoughts have to do with anything? Everything! What we expect to see, we see. What we expect to have in our lives, we have. What we focus on the most, expands.

If your life isn't what you want it to be, your thoughts have not been in alignment with it. This can be a tricky concept to understand, but the most important point to get is that it's a cumulative process.

Think of a scale. If you place a grain of sand in one of the trays, it probably won't make much difference to the balance of the scale. But if you add another grain, and another, and another, before long the scale will begin to tilt in that direction. Your thoughts work in much the same way, and if you have enough of one particular type of thought, it will affect your quality of life.

This may sound bad, but it's actually a good thing! If we can create imbalance and lack with our thoughts and habits, we can also create abundance and success. It's all within our control.

What if I told you that just by changing your mind-set, you could begin to effortlessly attract the success you desire? What if you could not only attract success, but become successful at a core level?

You can! By following the techniques in this book, you will learn how to transform your thinking processes and develop a true success mind-set. And with the right mind- set, there is no limit to what you can create in your life.

The important thing to remember as you embark upon this journey is that it's a process. Take your time and enjoy it. Don't expect perfection – simply relax and have fun with the techniques! Trust me, they will work much better if you have fun with them, rather than getting mired in frustration or placing unrealistic expectations on yourself. Remember that a large part of success is the contentment you feel in each moment. Allow yourself to feel it now, even if everything in your life isn't the way you wish it were. Soon enough, it will be.

Wishing you a smooth transition to the success you deserve.

Happiness: Cause or Effect?

Are you happy with your life the way it is now? There are probably aspects of your life you'd like to change, otherwise you wouldn't be reading this book. But overall, can you say you're truly happy? Most of us can't, but it's not because we're still seeking success. Rather, we aren't happy because we haven't made the choice to be happy.

When we think of being successful, we imagine that happiness is an inevitable side effect. We may envision ourselves with the perfect job, the perfect mate, the perfect children, the perfect level of income, the perfect home, the perfect car, etc. And we believe that all of that stuff will make us happy.

However, that view is skewed. Material objects and other people cannot make us happy – only we can make ourselves happy. And it all begins with a choice to be happy.

You probably don't believe that, especially if you are experiencing challenges or lack in your life right now. But think about this: *why do rich people still experience unhappiness?*

Why do successful people still experience unhappiness? Because money and success do not automatically create happiness!

Neither do power, status, romance, or material objects. We simply believe they do because we are looking outside of ourselves for the solution to our problems.

> *Before everything else, getting ready is the secret of success*
>
> **– Henry Ford**

The Truth about Money and Happiness

Intellectually, we may know that money can't buy happiness, but some part of us still believes that we'd feel better if we were rich. Yet when we really look at wealthy people, we must wonder if they are any happier than the average person. Do wealthy people laugh more, experience more joy, or have greater fulfillment in their lives? Perhaps some do – but how much of it is a direct result of their wealth?

In fact, you can probably point to a handful of wealthy people that appear to be completely miserable. Not surprisingly, some people seem to become less satisfied the wealthier they become! Perhaps they were under the misconception that money would solve all their problems, or having a large amount of money brought along its own challenges. I'm sure you've heard the horror stories about people who win the lottery or come into a large sum of money through an inheritance or other means. Many of them experience a few years of heartache and struggle, and end up flat broke again. Money didn't solve their problems – only made them worse!

Another reason why wealth can make us miserable is that it distracts us from what is truly important for a happy and fulfilling life. We find ourselves focusing more and more on material objects and end up feeling disconnected from our inner selves.

If you are feeling unhappy in your life right now and you're thinking that money will solve your problems, it's time for a reality check! I won't deny that having material abundance can make our lives a little easier. Believe me, I'm all too aware of what it's like to struggle to pay the bills or feel like you're living on the edge of a cliff and the ground is crumbling beneath your feet. I know the terror of worrying whether the electricity will be shut off for nonpayment or wondering if you'll be able to afford to buy groceries this week.

I'm not trying to minimize these types of struggles – but I want you to be clear that having a lot of money will not automatically. Make you feel happy and content in your life.

Money can definitely help us to enjoy a greater quality of life, but only if we have a healthy attitude toward money; otherwise, it will just add bigger burdens.

A Genuine Sense of Security

One reason we're so focused on wealth acquisition is the need to feel secure. We believe that if we have a large amount of money in the bank, we'll be protected from lack, pain, difficulty and struggle. In a limited sense this is true. However, security is simply a state of mind!

It's not the money itself that makes us feel secure; **it's our belief that adequate financial reserves protect us from bad experiences.**

If we look logically at this concept, we realize that having a lot of money really can't protect us from anything, except perhaps surprise expenses. Still, a fat bank account doesn't guarantee we'll never experience anything negative. There will always be car accidents, terror attacks, illness, job loss, troublesome relationships, and more. Having a lot of money won't matter when we find ourselves in those situations, because they are completely out of our control.

The only true security we have is what we can create in our own minds. There is true security in believing in ourselves, in having confidence to overcome challenges, in our spiritual beliefs, and in doing our small part to make this world a better place.

Imagine living your life with the unshakable belief that you have what it takes to succeed, no matter what else is happening around you? Imagine never feeling frightened by outside influences again. Imagine knowing that even if the worst case scenario were to happen, you could easily and quickly pull yourself up by the bootstraps and do what needed to be done to get back on track.

That's true security

Believing in our ability to handle whatever comes our way is much more effective than trying to guard against potential negative experiences. That's the best kind of security, because it empowers us to feel in control of our lives – if not every situation, at least the outcome of the bigger picture.

The Quest for Empowerment

Another way we try to create a sense of security in our lives is by seeking power. We believe that if we obtain a position of power, happiness and success will automatically follow.

Power, just like security, is an illusion. It can't prevent us from experiencing anything negative. It can't erase our deep-seated feelings of inadequacy or insecurity. It can't make us successful.

In fact, power over others often becomes a burden all its own! Along with the ability to control people and situations come the responsibilities and obligations that flank a position of power.

Rather than feeling in control, we feel more out of control than ever.

As much as we might like to, we can't control certain events in our lives, and we can't control others. We can control only our own thoughts and actions.

What most of us are really seeking is a sense of EMPOWERMENT. Not control over others, not control over outside circumstances, but control over our own thoughts, emotions, and actions.

As frightening as it may seem to release the illusion of power, it's also very freeing in a way. Once we "get it" that we don't HAVE to be in control of anything except ourselves, we learn to relax and let go of what we have no control of. We learn to go with the flow and do our best without trying.

To meet some vague, impossible standards we set for ourselves in an effort to feel in control.

Dissolving Emotional Blockages

Even if all outer aspects of our lives seem wonderful, our emotions can still cause us to feel unhappy. Traumatic memories can stifle our development. Negative thought habits can fill us with feelings of frustration and powerlessness. Negative self-talk can cause us to sabotage any goals we set.

Emotions can be a tricky thing to understand, but it becomes easier when we consider that our emotions are fueled by our thoughts.

If we THINK negatively about ourselves, we will FEEL badly about ourselves.

If we focus on the negative in our lives, our lives will seem to have a negative theme. It's all about what we focus on the most that determines how we feel.

Think about the last time your day took a sudden nosedive because of something simple.

Let's say you were driving to work, singing along with a song on the radio, and some jerk cut you off in traffic. Your first thought might be, "What a jerk!" (Or a more colorful term) Your next thought might be, "People are so rude these days, and I seem to encounter the rudest of them all! What did I ever do to deserve this?"

From there your mood can continue to spiral down as you ponder your bad luck in having to deal with inconsiderate people.

Do you see what happens in situations like these? You have a negative experience, and then you internalize it. Not just for the moment either, but for the rest of your day. Even worse, because your attitude tends to attract most of your experiences, feeling negative will continue to attract more rude and inconsiderate people into your day.

Though it seems impossible, we can control our emotions. We can choose our emotions, moment to moment. And we begin by choosing our thoughts. Using the example from above, what would be a more empowering response? You could simply say, "That wasn't very nice," and then turn your attention back to the song you were singing.

That may seem like a difficult thing to do when your anger is ignited, but with practice it gets easier. Rather than internalizing the things that happen to you (especially things you can't control), simply let go of them and keep your emotional balance. If you pay attention to how you feel throughout the course of your day, you'll become aware of whether your thoughts are negative or positive. Then you can simply choose to release your negative thoughts and replace them with positive thoughts – which will make you feel better. Again, it takes consistent effort to fully master this technique.

Releasing the Past to Make Room for Something Better

Letting go of past traumas is a little more challenging because they are often buried.

Deeply in our subconscious minds. But buried or not, they can still wreak havoc on our level of happiness.

One of the most powerful techniques I've learned for releasing old baggage is to relive the painful experiences. It doesn't sound like much fun (and in fact it isn't) but it is definitely freeing. If you stop to think about it, much of our emotional baggage is "buried" simply because we didn't allow ourselves to work through it the first time around. We squelched down the feelings and tried to ignore them, and there they still lie, festering. If we unearth the painful memories and work through them like we could have done when they originally happened, we are able to release them and achieve closure.

This is a simple process you can undertake on your own, but if you've had very large, life-altering traumas, you may want to consult a counselor or therapist to help you work through them. While the process is simple, it can be emotionally overwhelming, and having a trained professional as a guide can provide invaluable support.

Once you've worked through your emotional blockages, you may also want to examine the underlying beliefs that formed because of them.

For example, an abusive childhood might result in a deep-seated belief that you're not worthy of being loved. Working through painful memories can be freeing, but it won't automatically change your underlying.

Beliefs about your worthiness as a human being. You could still find yourself avoiding intimacy and sabotaging your efforts to create a fulfilling life.

The good news is that once you identify your limiting beliefs, you can begin charging them with a little conscious focus.

> *To bring one's self to a frame of mind and to the proper energy to accomplish things that require plain hard work continuously is the one big battle that everyone has. When this battle is won for all time, then everything is easy."*
>
> **Thomas A. Buckner**

Transforming Limiting Beliefs into Empowering Beliefs

Changing your existing beliefs is a simple process. The only thing you need is the determination to keep at it until it "clicks" in your mind.

To start with, try these three steps:

1. **Replace negative thoughts with positive ones.** While positive thinking alone will not alter your existing beliefs, it is a practice that can help you get in line with your thought patterns in a more conscious way. Rather than being a victim of your own thoughts, you can take control of them and choose them moment-to-moment. As you become aware of negative thoughts throughout the day, consciously replace them with equally positive (and usually opposite) thoughts.

   For example, if you find yourself thinking that you'll never be successful because you just can't seem to break out of your limiting behaviors, consciously affirm that you have just as much potential to be successful as anyone else.

   Visualize yourself with the determination, courage, and optimism you'll need to succeed. And the next time negative thoughts arise in your mind, go through the same process again.

Remember that it is a process, and it will take time to get into the habit of thinking positively, but it does begin to have an effect on how you feel on a regular basis. And the better you feel, the more positively.

You'll think. You end up creating a continuous cycle of positive thoughts, positive feelings, positive beliefs, and positive actions!

2. **Develop a stronger belief in yourself.** While you're working on transforming the quality of your thoughts, you can also purposely develop a strong belief in yourself and your abilities. A good way to start is by making a list of your positive character traits, qualities, skills, and talents. Write down every positive thing you can come up with about yourself, even if you don't think it's that amazing.

Then simply spend some time every day reading this list and affirming your ability to accomplish whatever you set your mind to. Over time, you'll begin to feel more positive about yourself and more confident about your abilities, just because you've developed the habit to do so.

3. **Empower and motivate yourself.** Another wonderful tool for forming new beliefs is using your imagination to change your

self-image. Visualization is an easy yet effective tool to replace your old, limiting self-image with an empowering new one. You simply close your eyes and conjure a mental image of yourself as you want to be.

See yourself feeling confident, inspired, courageous, and successful. Before long, you'll find that you won't have to manufacture these feelings; you will feel this way nearly all the time – naturally!

Again, this exercise is most effective if you do it every day, even for just a few minutes.

The Keys to Happiness

We already know that basing our happiness on external circumstances can be tenuous at best. So what does create feelings of happiness? Happiness is a personal concept that is probably different for each of us. Take a moment to consider what happiness means to you. That's one important step in understanding how you can bring more happiness into your life.

Think about the people, places, and things that fill you with joy and peace. Do you feel happiest when you're at home, or at work? How about when you're spending time with friends and loved ones? Or when you're reading an uplifting book, watching a funny movie, or donating your time to help others? Whatever activities you enjoy the most, make an effort to bring more of them into your life.

It's easy for us to sabotage ourselves by placing restrictions on our happiness. We affirm that we'll be happy if this happens, or that happens, but not when the other happens. Of course, certain situations just aren't pleasant no matter what – but for the most part, we can choose to enjoy most of our experiences and outcomes, even if they aren't what we originally expected.

Beyond all of this, however, most important is our willingness to accept that happiness is largely a choice we make in every moment, regardless of our surroundings. Happiness is not a gift we're waiting for; it's already within us. All we need to do is choose to embrace it; which can be easier said than done, especially if we're in the midst of difficult circumstances. The true skill we should be strengthening within ourselves is learning how to be happy on a basic level, even if our lives aren't perfect. By acknowledging that our lives will never be "perfect," we give ourselves permission to enjoy our lives as they are now.

When it comes right down to it, I think Abraham Lincoln said it best: "Most people are about as happy as they make up their minds to be."

Learning How to Love Yourself

You may wonder what self-love has to do with success. The answer is: more than you can imagine! Self-love and self-worth go hand in hand. If we don't believe we're worthy of success, we'll keep pushing it away or find ways to sabotage ourselves from achieving it.

Our self-image is formed from a set of inner beliefs about ourselves. These beliefs are based upon past experiences and what we determined they meant at the time.

Exploring the beliefs that form your self- image is important because they will determine your thoughts, feelings, behaviors – and ultimately your level of success in ALL things.

Have you ever uttered statements like these? "I stink at math."

"I'm terrified of public speaking." "I could never be an airplane pilot."

"I don't have what it takes to be successful." "I'm just not a people person."

"No matter what I do, I can't seem to get ahead."

It's very easy to buy into these "excuses" (yes, that's what they are!) because they remove the responsibility from our shoulders. Convincing ourselves that we're just "not good" at something means we no longer have to try hard or take risks. It's out of our hands. Consequently, we end up holding ourselves back from the lives we really wish we were living. We end up feeling stuck in a cycle of frustration, wanting something better but not believing we have the ability to create it.

Overcoming Negative Preconceptions

In order to break free from limiting beliefs, we need to change our preconceptions.

Preconceptions are previously formed opinions or ideas we hold about ourselves. These beliefs have the power to influence how we feel about ourselves, what we believe we are capable of, and the actions we take (or don't take) to create the life we want.

So how do we overcome these negative preconceptions? Just like changing our negative thinking to positive, it takes consistent effort and focus.

Changing our negative self-talk into positive self-talk on a consistent basis is key.

Rather than tearing ourselves down, we can choose to fill our inner dialogue with empowering affirmations and build ourselves up.

Think about this: how would you speak to someone you loved and respected?

Would you be cruel and unforgiving? Or would you be kind, encouraging and supportive? It doesn't matter what others say to you, or how others treat you. What matters is how you treat yourself! (Ironically, the better you treat yourself, others pick up on that and begin to see you differently – and ultimately treat you better. It's all about what you believe you deserve.)

At the same time, you can also shift your focus from what you don't want, to what you DO want.

For example, if you fear failure you are motivated to avoid failure at all costs (which usually means procrastinating on your goals and avoiding risk-taking). If you instead focus most of your attention on being successful at whatever you do, you'll find that the fear of failure diminishes.

The more you focus on what you WANT, the less you will attract what you DON'T WANT.

> *Man is still responsible. ... His success lies not with the stars, but with himself. He must carry on the fight of self-correction and discipline.*
>
> **– Frank Curtis Williams**

Getting to Know Yourself

It's so ironic that we usually avoid the very thing that would help us build a strong foundation of confidence and self-esteem: spending time with ourselves.

How does that help anything?

Getting to know yourself can blast through any negative preconceptions you may be harboring. Remember, your self-image is usually based on the conclusions you formed from your past experiences. You may hold a belief that you are not a good writer, or you're not a "people person", or that you don't have any special skills, but is that really true? How do you know for sure?

Please don't say, "Because I tried it once and I sucked at it." Trying something once (or only a few times) doesn't count.

The truth is, you can become good (or even great) at anything if you want it badly enough and you're willing to put in the time and effort to get there.

Here's the million-dollar question: Do you really want to get "there"? Getting to know yourself helps you separate what YOU really want from what others expect of you. You might think you want to be a great writer because your mother praised the short story you wrote in sixth grade.

You craved her approval, so your desire to be a writer might be all wrapped up in the illusion of receiving praise and recognition. You don't want to write, you just want to be a "great writer." If you constantly procrastinate on writing and can't seem to push yourself to do it, you might want to question whether you really want to be a writer after all. Perhaps your true passion lies elsewhere. That is just one example of the many ways we can deceive ourselves.

If you take time to get to know yourself – REALLY know yourself – you will discover things that were previously hidden (or denied because they didn't match others' expectations of you).

Here is the best and quickest way to get to know yourself: spend time alone as often as possible. Shut off the television and radio, block outside distractions, and simply allow yourself to BE.

If this suggestion sounds frightening or intimidating to you, it's a sure sign that you are NOT in touch with your inner self. If you were, you'd know that there is nothing to fear about spending time with yourself – in fact you would be excited at the prospect of doing so!

As soon as possible, begin a new habit that can change your life in dramatic ways: begin spending some quiet, quality time with yourself each day. If you feel intimidated, start small with increments of just ten minutes or so. Sit quietly in a private place and let your thoughts flow naturally. Think about yourself, who you are, what you feel passionate about, what you want out of life, the things you've accomplished, the things you want to accomplish, your relationships – whatever comes to mind.

The more you do this, the more connected you become to your inner self. You begin to tap into your inner dialogue, and a deeper understanding of yourself will surface. The changes you experience from this process might seem small at first, but they quickly gain momentum.

Another good exercise to get to know yourself is journaling. Get a lined, spiral bound notebook and start recording your thoughts during your quiet time alone. Don't worry about spelling, grammar or context. If you understand your scribbles, that's all that matters. Write down your thoughts, feelings, struggles, fears, and dreams. Draw pictures. Ask yourself questions and answer them. Vent your frustrations and strengthen your resolve to do better. It doesn't matter WHAT you write really, just that you connect with yourself genuinely and frequently.

Falling in Love with Your Uniqueness

Getting to know yourself if one important part of the growth process, but equally important is loving and appreciating yourself. Self-deprecation is a habit, just like all types of negative thinking.

Unless you begin to appreciate your strengths, believe in yourself and reinforce your true capabilities, you will not move forward in life! Sure, you might stumble across the random opportunity and make some progress occasionally, but you won't accidentally achieve the level of success you desire.

First and foremost, choose to forgive yourself NOW. Forgive yourself for anything you may feel guilty about, for allowing fear to hold you back from what you really want to do, for not believing in yourself, for allowing other people to define you. Affirm that you did the best you knew how to do, but now you know better – and will do better.

Stop the cycle of self-abuse and begin honoring yourself for the beautiful and brilliant person you were meant to be.

Begin a habit of encouraging yourself. Speak kindly to yourself and affirm your ability to accomplish anything you want. Eventually, you will begin to believe it.

At the same time, work on forgiving anyone who has harmed you, belittled you or held you back. Even though these experiences may have affected you in profound ways, they do not have the ability to affect you now – unless you choose to let them.

Let go of your anger, hurt, disappointment and bitterness. They do not serve you, and they do not punish the guilty. They only punish you by acting as a heavy weight bearing down upon your shoulders. If you release them, you free yourself to create the joy and success you truly deserve.

Starting now, choose to believe in yourself and your abilities. Believe that you can form your life into anything you want it to be. Believe that you can overcome any obstacle, strengthen any skill, tackle any challenge and conquer any fear you may have. The more strongly believe you can do it, the more likely it is that you WILL.

It really is a CHOICE!

Creating Meaningful Work

Does your work make you happy? Or are you simply trading hours for dollars doing something you couldn't care less about?

Meaningful work means different things to different people.

Some of us believe that in order for our work to be meaningful it must have a huge impact on the world. Discovering a cure for cancer, feeding millions of starving children around the world, or protecting endangered species are good examples of what most people would consider meaningful work. But is that all? What if our passions lie elsewhere? Can any type of work be meaningful?

Yes – to those who benefit from it!

Consider an alternate definition of meaningful work: something that you feel passionate about, which also provides value to the world.

Any type of job or career can be valuable, if you think about it. Doctors, lawyers, accountants, caterers, musicians, artists, housekeepers, dog walkers, party planners, product manufacturers, hair stylists – they are ALL providing something of value.

In that sense, any job at all can be meaningful. But is it meaningful to YOU?

This is where a lot of people go wrong, by choosing work that "has meaning" but is not exactly meaningful to them.

Perhaps your high school guidance counselor convinced you to go into medicine, but your true passion is music. Or your father was a lawyer, so you felt obligated to follow in his footsteps. Or you weren't sure what to study in college, so you picked a field that seemed simple and paid well but now you feel bored.

You may not think it matters what you do, as long as you're able to pay the bills. Or you may be a "weekend warrior," devoting weekdays to a mundane job and following your passions on the weekends.

There is nothing wrong with this if it makes you feel happy and fulfilled. But if you walk around with a constant feeling of frustration and emptiness, you might want to re-evaluate your career path and choose something that truly fulfills you.

> *The very first step towards success in any occupation is to become interested in it*
>
> *– **Sir William Oslar***

Doing What You Love for a Living

What were your dreams when you were a child?

Did you dream of being a heroic firefighter? A famous singer? President of the United States?

What happened to those dreams? If you're like most people, you were told how unrealistic your dreams were and you were encouraged to be more practical. "Get a real job" is the phrase many of us heard from parents, teachers and other authority figures in our lives.

If you have buried those long-ago dreams so deeply in your subconscious mind that you can no longer even remember them, don't despair! A little introspection can help bring them to the surface, but even if they remain hidden, there is one important thing to remember:

You are not the same person now that you were back then!

While it is possible to rekindle a dream you've held since childhood, you do not have to. Instead, let new dreams make themselves known to you. Ask yourself what type of work would make you feel most fulfilled. Ask yourself how you can best make a contribution to the world by doing something you truly love.

It sounds simple in theory, but how do you start? Many of us have fallen completely out of touch with our passions. We're so focused on the things we HAVE to do that we have no time for play or exploration.

I'm going to be blunt with you: there is no other alternative but to MAKE time. Set aside some time to really get to know yourself. Figure out what you like to do or explore new activities so you can decide whether they might be one of your true passions. You don't have to devote dozens of hours to this, perhaps start with 30-60 minutes a day.

Identifying and Nurturing Your Talents

A good place to start is by gaining a clear idea of your skills and talents. Make a list of the things you are naturally good at, as well as the things you've become good at through repetitive effort. Write down the skills you use in your job, the things you learned in school, and the things you enjoy doing in your spare time.

When you've listed everything you can, look over your list and consider whether any of these skills and talents might be marketable. How can you use your talents to provide something of value to others?

Take your time with this exercise!

Seriously, don't rush through it. You're trying to get an idea of the work that would make you feel passionate and fulfilled – therefore it deserves your undivided attention.

This exercise is also important for another reason. Your dream is NOT just about you. It's about all the lives you will touch when you do what you were meant to do on this planet. It took me a long time to understand that by holding myself back I was denying others something special I had to share with them. And I don't mean that as a boast.

We are each special and unique, and we each have something to offer this world that no one else does. By denying our own talents, we deny others the gift of what we have to share.

So please, don't skimp on this exercise. You owe it to yourself and others to be ruthlessly honest about your passion(s).

Once you have a clear list of your existing skills and talents, make a check mark next to the ones you use on a regular basis, whether in your work or personal time. Can any of those skills be enhanced or strengthened? Can you enroll in a continuing education course to expand on any of your skills? Make notes about possible opportunities to grow and develop what you already have.

(Note: if any of the skills on your list are not things you truly ENJOY doing, cross them off the list and do not consider them as career candidates. That doesn't mean you'll never use those skills, just that they won't be your main focus. A good example might be bookkeeping or accounting skills that you use in your day job. You may be good with numbers but if working with them doesn't thrill you and move you, you should simply consider it an additional tool that can help with your work.)

What's left on your list? Look at the talents that were not checked as something you use frequently. Would you like to spend more time developing those talents? Again, if they don't thrill you, cross them off the list. If they do interest you, consider ways to expand and develop them further.

Finally, make one more list: of things you've always wanted to do but haven't yet. These will be things you can explore gradually and see if they have potential to be your passion.

Then, be sure to MAKE TIME to explore them! Check out courses and classes in your local area, or do a few internet searches for groups of likeminded people. Give your interests a chance, and one (or more) of them might blossom into a life- changing passion.

Learning How to Work Smart – Not Just Hard!

Many of us fall into the trap of believing that becoming successful will require a lot of hard work. While hard work can be good for us, too much of it can create the opposite effect we're going for. Think about it: we crave fulfilling work because we want to enjoy our daily lives, not feel exhausted or bored. Taking hard work to the extreme only holds us back, personally and professionally.

Contrary to what you may have been taught, hard work alone has little (if nothing) to do with success. Think about people who are working long hours at low- paying jobs every day. Are they becoming successful because of their hard work? Or are they simply scraping by, paycheck to paycheck – as so many of us do?

Simply working hard is not the answer to becoming successful. Working steadily in a FOCUSED direction is. That's why I led you through all that "identifying your talents" stuff at the beginning of this chapter. If you don't know what you're working toward, you will be spinning your wheels no matter how hard you work.

Once you know your objective (passionate, fulfilling work that contributes value to the world), it is easy to come up with focused action steps that will make it a reality.

Working hard in THAT context can be extremely effective. You know where you're going, you know exactly what to do to get there, and all you need is the discipline and determination to see it through.

We'll explore taking action more completely in a later chapter.

Making Time for What Really Matters

It is crucial to avoid getting caught in the trap of all work and no play. Often when our dream is big, or it has been a part of us for a very long time, we become consumed by it. We trick ourselves into believing that sacrificing our relationships and family time in order to achieve our goals will pay off in the long run – but sadly, this is rarely true.

Instead, keeping a healthy balance between work and play automatically helps us feel energetic and enthusiastic, therefore we are less stressed, and therefore our focus becomes sharper, and we get more done in less time.

Think about it this way: whatever you focus on the most expands, and whatever you turn your focus away from shrivels and dies.

That may be the reason you don't feel like you have achieved the success you desire; because you have not given your career path the focus it deserves. Likewise, if your relationships are lacking, or you struggle with financial strain, or your health and fitness leaves something to be desired. It works the same in all areas of your life. Everything needs nurturing to help it grow.

So, believing that it won't matter if you neglect the other areas of your life while you are actively pursuing success is a grave mistake.

If you make a conscious effort to see all aspects of your life as an INVESTMENT in your productivity, you will reap great rewards! What do I mean by investment?

The time you take to care for yourself, build strong relationships with your family and friends, and recharge your mental and physical batteries will DIRECTLY affect your ability to succeed at anything else in life. Not only will you feel happier and more centered on a daily basis, you won't grow to resent your passion because it sucks the life out of you.

You will accomplish more in less time with short, focused bursts of activity, rather than depleting your energy with longer, watered-down work sessions.

Take it from someone who learned the hard way: less is more. Be reasonable about the amount of time you devote to your passion(s) and leave room for your other priorities. You'll enjoy the journey to success much more.

> *If I had known what it would be like to have it all, I might have been willing to settle for less.*
>
> *– Lily Tomlin*

Show Me the Money

Finally, I'd like to end this chapter by revisiting something we covered in the first chapter of this book.

IT'S NOT ABOUT THE MONEY!

Just as happiness is not about money, neither is success about money. Do yourself a favor and:

1. Don't choose your passion because of the money it can bring you.
2. Don't overwork and exhaust yourself in an effort to earn more money.
3. Don't focus on what you stand to gain from sharing your passion with the world.

Such requests may sound counterproductive since abundant financial rewards are undoubtedly one indication of success.

Read that last sentence again, especially the part that reads, "… **abundant financial rewards are undoubtedly ONE INDICATION of success."**

Did you get that? Money does not guarantee success, but is rather a side- effect of success (and a rather welcome one, at that!).

The reason I don't want you to focus on the money angle is because it will dilute your focus. You begin worrying about what you will "get" rather than what you can contribute to others. That might not seem like a big deal, but it is.

There is an old saying that everything you do is infused with your energy. We might clarify that to say everything you do is infused with the QUALITY of your energy. Think about this for a moment and you'll realize the truth of such a statement.

Have you ever done a task out of sheer obligation but your heart wasn't in it? Perhaps you wrote a report for school, or completed a project at work, or even attended an event because your spouse wanted to go but you had zero interest in it.

What happened with those activities? The report or project was likely passable as far as quality goes, but it probably didn't have any "oomph" did it? And what of the event you attend for someone else's benefit? You probably spent the majority of time bored out of your mind and didn't take anything valuable away from the experience.

There's a good reason for this: **you did not put forth high quality energy, so you ended up with lukewarm results. And the same thing will happen with your level of success!**

You might be thinking, "Great! If I put a lot of energy into the thought of money, I'll get a lot of money back!" Actually, no. It's not about the specific thoughts you are thinking, but the quality of ENERGY you are putting out.

If you focus on what you stand to gain, you are detracting from what you plan to give. That means that you are not putting anything of value out there into the world, and you will therefore experience lackluster results with whatever you do.

Ask yourself why successful people all seem to passionately love what they do for a living, and you'll be moving in the right direction!

Developing a True Success Mind

Set Have you ever observed successful people? Think about in-demand movie stars, business professionals, politicians, or any person in a position of power and affluence.

What quality or qualities do they all seem to have?

- Confidence
- Determination
- Discipline
- Focus
- Self-Worth
- Self-Esteem
- Self-Assurance

- Creativity
- Flexibility
- Resiliency
- Vision
- Patience
- Courage
- Self-Sufficiency

Which of these qualities do YOU have?

You might be able to check off one or two (or perhaps a few) of these qualities and call them your own, but you might struggle with the rest. Most people do, until they understand the foundation of success: developing a belief in yourself.

Developing A Belief in Yourself

That is the root from which all of the above qualities stem, and it is the same root from which success grows.

If you don't believe in yourself, if you don't believe you deserve to be successful, if you don't believe that you have what it takes to create the successful life you crave – you will remain exactly where you are right now.

You may be thinking, "Okay, I get it, I need to believe in myself in order to be successful. But how am I supposed to believe in myself when I really DON'T believe in myself?!"

It seems like an impossible challenge, but once you begin making small changes in your mental and physical environments, you will be surprised how quickly your circumstances begin to shift.

Self-Belief Affirmations

Whether you are fighting your fear of the unknown future, fear of failure, rejection, or being judged, you'll find these positive statements helpful in dealing with all that and more.

Read through the affirmations below and find several that make the most sense to you right now. Repeat them as much as you need every day until you feel confident that your fear doesn't have control over you anymore. And then some.

Shifting affirmations are powerful, positive statements that can help you change your mindset, beliefs, and ultimately, your life. By focusing on your desired outcomes and repeating these affirmations, you can shift your mindset and attract positive experiences into your life.

> *A* man can do only *what* he can do. But if he does *that* each day he can sleep *at night and* do it *again the next day.*
>
> **Albert Schweitzer.**

Taking Responsibility for Where You Are Now

The first step in developing a true success mind-set is often the most painful, but it is also the most necessary. Before you can move forward, you need to understand that where you sit right now is no one's doing but your own.

That's not fun to hear, I know. You might be inclined to argue with me and point to any number of horrible, debilitating challenges you may have faced in your lifetime, and you may further argue that they damaged you beyond repair, forever limiting what you are capable of achieving.

I won't presume to tell you that these experiences don't matter, or that you are weak for letting them hold you back. I won't dare try to belittle the pain and struggle you have faced, because I know firsthand how paralyzing fear and pain can be.

However – it's important that you understand something about these challenges. They have not made you who you are today, and they have not determined the level of achievement you have reached in your life thus far.

It is only your perception of these events that matters!

It's not what happens to you that is important, only what you choose to do with the experiences and the conclusions you draw about yourself because of them.

Let's use a common example to demonstrate this point. If your mother was highly critical and constantly belittled you and everything you did, you might now have a belief that you are no good, that everything you do is worthless, and that you will never be successful at anything.

Is such a thing true? Yes, if you agree with it and internalize it.

But what if you decided not to believe it anymore? What if you decided to prove your mother wrong? What if you made a promise to yourself that you will persevere, no matter what else happens to you? What if you decided to stop focusing on your "flaws" and instead worked on building your strengths?

It is all within your control.

Do you realize that there are people in the world who have survived absolutely horrific experiences, and then went on to become multi-millionaires, set new world records, and positively affect millions of lives?

Why can't you do the same?

You absolutely can – if you stop using your challenges as an excuse not to try.

The whole point of taking responsibility for where you are now is to stop believing that you would have been more successful if you hadn't faced challenges in life, and acknowledge that you could have excelled.

IN SPITE of your challenges (and you still can!).

However, don't beat yourself up over this insight. Taking responsibility is not about abusing or browbeating yourself into doing better. Simply admit that you could have done better if you'd known how, and you will begin to try harder beginning right NOW.

Making the Right Choices, Moment to Moment

A common misconception that many of us share is the belief that success is a cohesive state of being that we will eventually claim as our own. In other words, we are under the false impression that we will one day take a giant leap from unsuccessful and frustrated to rich, happy and successful.

It may surprise you to learn that success is instead a process of making the right choices. It rarely (if ever) happens in one fell swoop. Rather, you go from making mostly poor or destructive choices to making better choices more often.

Take a look at the three stages below, and note the progression of a success-mindset:

Poor Choices	Results
- Procrastination	- Lack
- Self-doubt	- Stagnation
- Defeatism	- Frustration
- Resignation	- Victim mind-set
Better Choices	**Results**
- Self-belief	- Growing confidence
- Trust	- Optimism
- Hope	- Exhilaration
- Taking small actions	- Eagerness for more
Still Better Choices	**Results**
Building confidence	- Greater progress
Believing in abilities	- Accomplishment
Taking Bigger actions	- Deepening belief in oneself
Identifying true passions	- Freedom
Willingness to risk more	- Growing SUCCESS!

Again, this is a PROCESS. It is virtually impossible to start with a mind-set of lack and powerlessness and leap immediately to a mind-set of success and accomplishment.

Right now you may be feeling that it will take forever to get where you want to go in life. You may feel that the challenge is too big, the road is too rocky, and the obstacles are too intimidating. Not so!

Luckily for us, this type of process creates its own momentum. We start by making small changes both mentally and physically. We begin strengthening our desire for more, believing in ourselves and our capabilities, and taking small steps toward the lives we truly desire – and BOOM! More and more opportunities begin to appear before us.

As we grow in confidence, we begin NATURALLY gravitating toward choices that will support our deepest desires. We begin feeling an urge to do the things we know will create success, rather than shying away from them as we did in the past.

Do yourself a favor and avoid looking at the big picture, at least while you are just getting started. Instead, narrow your focus so you are looking at each teeny, tiny step you take along the path to success. Focus ONLY on these little steps and remind yourself that every decision you make (no matter how small or inconsequential it may seem) will serve to move you closer or farther away from your desired result.

Make a promise to yourself right now that you will begin listening to your intuition about which choices are right for you. Reinforce your awareness about how your actions determine your results, and vow to consistently make better and better choices until the process becomes more natural.

Question every move you are about to make. Ask yourself, "Will this help or hinder my ultimate objective?" Do this not only with every ACTION you contemplate taking, but also every INACTION you feel drawn to.

Keep in mind also that there are no right or wrong answers here, only what works best for you. For example, you may feel a desire to sit on the sofa and watch television for several hours in the evening. This can be both a positive and negative choice.

If you feel burned out from working too hard and need some downtime, taking a break is a positive choice.

If you are procrastinating on taking action and using the television as a distraction, it's a destructive choice.

Again, use your intuition (listen to your gut feelings) to determine whether you are making choices that will make you successful. Brutal honesty with yourself will be required, I won't kid you. It is astounding how easily we can fool ourselves and justify destructive behavior.

The only person we hurt when we do this is ourselves. There are no "success police" that will force us to make better decisions. We will receive no citations for laziness and procrastination. (Actually, the results we experience are worse than any citation we could receive.) It is up to us what we do with our time and talents. It is up to YOU what YOU will do with YOUR time and talents!

Clear Out the Cobwebs and Make a Fresh Start

Want to make a great new start, right now? Begin by clearing out the cobwebs from every corner of your life!

You may not think your corners have cobwebs but I assure you, if you have been mired in negative, fear-based thinking for any length of time, your entire life is filled with stagnant energy that will continue to drain your power.

Clearing out the cobwebs is a very simple process of sweeping away old, stagnant situations that no longer serve you so you can make room for shiny new circumstances that DO. What do I mean by "stagnant situations"?

- Destructive or unfulfilling relationships, partnerships and friendships
- Boring or unchallenging jobs
- Unhealthy habits
- Unfinished business
- Unnecessary expenses
- Excessive obligations

These situations will vary greatly from person to person, and only you will know when it is time to let something go.

You might be in a marriage that has become a drag, but that doesn't mean you have to eliminate it unless you feel a need to do so. There are other options, like having a heartfelt talk with your partner and working on improving the relationship together.

Your job might be boring and unchallenging, but you balk at the thought of quitting without another job to take its place. That's okay! You don't have to quit, but at least give some thought to obtaining a better job that makes you feel happier.

The point of clearing out the cobwebs isn't to go on a "wrecking-ball rampage" through your life, but rather to **identify situations that are out of balance and in need of attention**. Once you have identified these areas, you can decide on the best course of action for each one.

Little by little, begin addressing any areas of stagnation or blockage in your life, and little by little you'll notice yourself FEELING BETTER. As your mood improves, so will your ability to look to the future with hope and enthusiasm, rather than dread and fear.

Special areas to pay attention to:

Work

Incomplete tasks and projects, overloaded schedule, cluttered office, unproductive habits, unresolved resentment, unhealthy work relationships, unclear objectives, lack of long-term planning.

Relationships

Unspoken truths, bitterness, unaddressed anger, grudges, guilt, regrets, dishonesty, destructive behavior, abuse, trust, passion, cooperation.

Financial

Increasing income, reducing unnecessary expenses, proper money management, long-term planning, saving and investing, budgeting, reducing debt, collecting monies owned to you.

Physical, Emotional, Spiritual

Poor health habits, excessive work, procrastination, work/life balance, recreational time with loved ones, proper rest and nutrition, anti-social tendencies, moodiness, anger, spiritual disconnection, inner emptiness, lack of purpose or direction, personal time, personal growth, self-improvement.

Do you see the importance of this process? It's like clearing a logjam out of the river so water can flow freely downstream again. If you clear the situations that are causing a blockage in your life, you will open the door to greater success and prosperity – in all areas of your life.

Allowing Yourself to Be Successful

Even without your conscious awareness, your current beliefs may be holding you back. Whether you struggle to believe in yourself, your capabilities, or the vast array of limitless possibilities for your life, you may be shutting out the very thoughts that can propel you to the success you desire.

Pause for a moment and answer this question: Can you really "see" yourself as a confident, successful person? If you close your eyes and call up an image of yourself, what does that self look like? Is he or she enthusiastic about life, willing to take risks, eager to grasp the joy and abundance he/she deserves? Can you imagine this person with endless opportunities for growth and advancement in life?

If you can't quite "see" yourself as being successful (or at least having the potential to be successful), it is likely that your own beliefs are creating an inner blockage.

Unless you turn this around and open your mind to what is possible, you will continue to sabotage your own efforts.

Dissolving inner blockages is not as difficult as it may seem. The two main things you need to have are: 1) the willingness to believe something different, and 2) the courage to take action on your new beliefs.

The first step requires a large dose of faith when you first begin to shift your beliefs. All of the "evidence" in your life seems to reinforce your current beliefs, right?

You believe you are not successful, not confident, not courageous enough to take risks, and perhaps not the "lucky" type of person that finds great opportunities to move forward.

If these are your beliefs, your outer life probably "proves" them to be accurate. You may struggle with lack, fear, procrastination, confusion and frustration on a daily basis. Therefore you know your beliefs are "true".

What many people fail to understand is that their beliefs are what create the "evidence" in their lives.

Here is how it usually happens:

As a child, you are naturally confident, optimistic, open-minded and ready to tackle challenges. You've got all the potential in the world at this point, and your life is a blank slate, waiting for you to turn it into a masterpiece. Then the negative conditioning begins. You are given conditions and limitations by the adults in your life (whether your parents, teachers, pastor, or other authority figures).

These conditions and limitations begin to alter your belief in what is possible for your life. Rather than encouraging your dream of becoming an astronaut (or whatever your personal dream is), you are scolded into being more "practical".

You start to believe that your dream is foolish, and you are foolish for believing in useless fantasies.

Even worse, the adults in your life start attaching limiting labels to you: learning disabled, dumb, unlucky, accident prone, head in the clouds, challenged, sensitive, weak-willed, irresponsible (and sometimes much more damaging ones).

Eventually, after you begin to believe these things, your actions are affected by them. Instead of choosing Path A, you move toward Path B because you just don't have what it takes to be one of the "elite" in life.

Throughout your lifetime, every decision you make is based on the beliefs you formed as a child and young adult.

Beliefs prompt specific actions which create specific results which reinforce the beliefs.

Changing your limiting beliefs requires a willingness to have faith that you are NOT dumb, challenged, irresponsible, weak-willed, or unlucky – even though your experiences thus far seem to have "proven" those things as being true.

But here's the good news: if you suspend your beliefs and dare to hope that maybe your impressions are false, and once you start taking actions that correspond with more positive beliefs, your results will change!

> *My mother said to me 'If you become a soldier, you'll be a general. If you become a monk, you'll end up as the Pope.' Instead, I became a painter and wound up as Picasso.*
>
> **– Pablo Picasso**

What Does Attitude Have to Do with Success?

One of my favorite old rhymes perfectly demonstrates the power of perception:

Two men peering through prison bars, One sees mud and the other sees stars.

One of these men is looking at the negative side of his situation. He looks out of his prison cell and, rather than seeing the beauty of the night sky he sees only the mud on the ground.

The other man ignores the mud and looks to the heavens, letting himself be inspired and dazzled by the display of light in the sky.

In other circumstances, which of these two men would you expect to become successful? If you think of success as a recipe with carefully measured portions of specific ingredients, attitude is one of those vital ingredients that give life to your concoction. It's like yeast added to a bread recipe to make the bread rise. Without yeast, your bread will end up flat, dense, and hard as a rock.

Likewise, a negative attitude will deflate your efforts to be successful. Why?

A positive attitude gives you the ability to overlook setbacks and continue toward your goals. It gives you the courage to tackle challenges and believe in yourself. It helps you keep obstacles in perspective, rather than feeling intimidated and giving up.

I'm sure you've heard the famous quote by Henry Ford, "Whether you think you can or think you can't, you're right."

It's all about perception!

If you knew for sure that there was no possible way for you to accomplish a goal, would you still try? Of course not. What would be the point?

If, on the other hand, you believed in your heart that you could achieve something, you'd be chomping at the bit to get started, and nothing would deter you!

Your attitude is what makes the difference in these two scenarios.

Developing a positive attitude is a simple matter of consistently training your brain to see the positive side of every situation.

Rather than peering at the mud, look to the stars. Rather than feeling powerless against challenges, affirm that you can get through them. Rather than letting other people determine what you are capable of – determine it yourself!

There is No Try, Only Do

We often think of failure as the inability to accomplish a certain objective. We give it our best shot and the results are less than favorable. We've failed.

Ah, but does that have to be the end of the story? No! We can consider it a failure ONLY if we stop trying after we experience the less than favorable result.

If we keep working at it, we might turn a "failure" into a success!

Do yourself a favor and change your definition of failure right now. Here is your new definition of failure:

Not having a plan, not working a plan, and giving up too soon.

Think of any great achievement in history, and you can be certain that the achiever had to attempt it more than once – sometimes hundreds of times!

If you've "failed" at anything in the past, be honest with yourself: how many times did you try? Did you give it a halfhearted effort and then give up when it seemed too hard? Did you let yourself become intimidated by challenges, or disempowered by negative comments from friends and colleagues?

Though you may believe that it was out of your hands, it's important to understand something:

You made a choice to fail.

You gave up. You stopped trying. It doesn't matter what the reasons were, even though they may have seemed perfectly logical at the time. The fact is, you allowed external conditions to erode your motivation and determination, and you threw in the towel.

You may resist this idea because let's face it; it's not a comfortable thing to hear. But this painful little insight comes with some good news!

If you made the choice to fail, you can also make the choice to succeed.

Whether you decide to pick up an old dream and dust it off or choose an exciting new path to travel, the outcome is within your control!

With the right attitude, focused action steps and a solemn vow to never give up, success will be yours.

Don't approach your goals with an attitude of "try," only an attitude of DO! That little gem by the fictional character of Yoda actually holds a tremendous amount of wisdom.

"Trying" means you are not going to give it your all. It means you will keep going until the going gets too tough. It means you are giving yourself an out in case you grow weary of the battle. It means you are giving yourself permission to surrender to mediocrity.

"Doing" means that failure is not an option. It means that you vow to give every ounce of blood, sweat and tears you have available because you believe in your dreams that much. It means that you cannot and will not accept defeat because the stakes are too high. It means that you are willing to work as long and as hard as necessary to achieve the outcome you desire, even if it takes years.

This is your life and you must decide that there is no going back, no giving up, no giving in – NO MATTER WHAT!

> *Let me tell you the secret that has led me to my goal. My strength lies solely in my tenacity.*
>
> *– Louis Pasteur*

The Joys and Evils of Expectations

Expectations can work for us, or against us. Expecting the best in every situation keeps us feeling motivated and passionate about our goals. Conversely, expecting immediate results from our efforts can make us feel frustrated and disappointed when it doesn't happen.

The tricky thing about expectations is that we may not always be aware of them on a conscious level. At some point during the pursuit of our goals we suddenly we find ourselves feeling angry, resentful or weary without a clear reason why. With a little introspection, we realize we've been holding unrealistic expectations about our progress, or fearfully expecting the worst in every situation.

Getting clear about your expectations – and consciously balancing them – can make your journey to success simple and painless.

How do you consciously balance an expectation? By NOT letting your emotions get attached to any one outcome.

"But wait a minute," you are probably thinking, "How can we not get attached to an outcome? Isn't that the whole point of having goals?"

When I say, "not getting attached to a specific outcome" I am not necessarily referring to your ultimate goal, but all the smaller milestones between here and there.

For example, one stumbling block our expectations can cause is related to timing. We crave success so badly that we pin our hopes on making it happen within 6 months (or one day!). If that doesn't happen, we get angry and feel like a failure.

If we didn't harbor unrealistic expectations about the timing of our success, we'd still be happily working on our goals. Instead, we sabotage ourselves by expecting too much, too soon.

See the difference? By consciously not getting attached to specific outcomes, you will be able to work consistently and steadily toward a goal, and make the journey much smoother!

This state of detachment can also be beneficial to your ultimate goal. Though you may have an idea of where you want to end up, would you be devastated if you ended up with a different (but equally good - or better) result? Chances are you would still feel an immense amount of satisfaction about your accomplishments.

It takes practice to feel comfortable balancing your expectations, but it gets easier as you go along. Eventually it will be second nature for you to remain optimistic yet realistic – which keeps you focused and motivated!

Here's how to start: with every goal you set, with every action step you take, every challenge you face, ask yourself, "What are my expectations for the outcome of this situation?"

If your expectations seem extreme in either direction (too optimistic or too pessimistic) – or too rigid altogether - adjust them accordingly. Only you can say for sure what is considered optimistic or pessimistic for YOU. It depends on your experience, determination, focus, and the magnitude of your goals. Something that would be extremely difficult for me might be a piece of cake for you. Consider your own abilities, set reasonable goals, and strive to challenge yourself – but not to the point where it seems like an exercise in futility and frustration!

Building Your Success Muscles with Discipline

If you are like most people, one of the biggest reasons you haven't yet achieved the success you desire is because you are not disciplined. In this age of instant gratification, we are accustomed to getting what we want right NOW. The thought of working diligently on a goal for weeks, months, or even years is a little depressing.

But without discipline, we are at the mercy of our circumstances and we will continue to be at their mercy. Once you get into a rut, you need tremendous discipline to pull yourself out of it.

One great example of this is being overweight and out of shape. If you've ever carried some extra pounds on your body, you know how exhausting and debilitating it can be. You feel sluggish, groggy, unmotivated – and the sofa seems like your best friend.

You know HOW to lose weight and get in shape: eat healthful food and exercise every day. But you don't do it. You make excuses about why you are overweight and sink further into lethargy because it seems too challenging to turn it around.

Then one day you decide you just can't stand feeling so rotten anymore, so you begin a diet and exercise plan. It's grueling hard work at the beginning. You need to give yourself constant pep talks to put on your workout clothes and get moving, and you need to ignore that little sweets monster that makes cookies seem so alluring.

The ONLY thing that determines your success in a scenario like this is your level of discipline. Will you keep doing what you know you need to do to lose weight? Will you push yourself to exercise? Will you continue to eat a balanced diet, or give in to your cravings for junk food?

This all sounds so unappealing, doesn't it?

Being disciplined is hard work.

Ah, but then something miraculous happens! If you keep at it for long enough, you begin to feel an inner shift. Suddenly you begin to realize that you are enjoying your workouts. You are beginning to look forward to your fruit smoothie each morning. Your clothes are getting baggy and your energy level is rising more each day. You are sleeping soundly at night and feeling better when you wake in the morning.

Amazingly, you don't need such a large amount of discipline to keep up with your health plan because it doesn't seem so difficult anymore. Your muscles are developing, your fat is melting away, and you are feeding your body a better quality of fuel, all of which make you feel so good that you want more. Cookies don't seem so powerful anymore. Even more importantly, you have become accustomed to your new habits! As long as you don't start backsliding, the rest of the journey to health and fitness is a rewarding joy ride.

This process is NO DIFFERENT for your goals, whatever they may be. It takes tremendous discipline at the beginning of the journey because you are not used to taking action on your goals. You will need to push yourself to do the things that need to be done.

Many of us give up at this stage because it seems too hard, and we believe it will ALWAYS be this hard. We forget that we humans are incredibly adaptive creatures. We can get used to almost anything.

Remember, we simply GOT USED to not trying. We settled into a state of acceptance about living a mediocre life, about abandoning our dreams, about believing the people who told us we'd never be successful.

If we can get used to THAT, we can get used to challenging ourselves, stretching our comfort zones, and believing in our own capabilities. It's just a matter of having the discipline and patience to see it through.

Make a solemn vow to yourself right now. Promise that you will keep taking action, keep working on improving yourself as a person, and keep striving for more happiness and success in whatever you do. Promise yourself that you will do what needs to be done on a daily basis – even if you don't feel like it.

If you can keep those promises, you will be astounded by the changes that take place in your life. (Remember, it's not an instant shift, so keep reminding yourself that it won't always be so difficult!) One of the sources I keep going back to is again, affirmations. At the end of this book I have additional pages with affirmations that can help you unlock your path to success in every area of your life.

Sacrifices: Making Room for What You Want

Sacrifice (like discipline) is one of those concepts that seems unappealing at first. We don't like to "give up" anything – especially not for the fleeting hope that it might be replaced with something better at an undetermined time in the future. Where's the fun in that?

Most of us yearn for the familiar and comfortable, even if it's dissatisfying. It seems less scary to stay safely ensconced in our routines. We avoid taking the actions we know we must take to be successful, because it seems easier not to. We sit in a vegetative state in front of the television so we don't have to think about how unhappy we are. And with each year that passes, we sink further into resignation.

I'm not going to ask you to give up the activities you love, such as watching television.

What I am going to do is ask you to consider what you would rather sacrifice. Either way, you are sacrificing SOMETHING. You are sacrificing your dreams as you hide your head in the sand, or you are sacrificing a portion of leisure time for a bigger goal.

Our perception of sacrifice is usually what makes it seem so unappealing. What can make it easier is a neat little trick I learned years ago: focus on what you are GAINING, not on what you are LOSING.

It's all about your perception!

If you think you have to be miserable now in order to be successful later, that's exactly how you'll end up feeling. If, on the other hand, you make a decision to feel happy about the changes you are making in your life, you will focus naturally on the benefits rather than the inconveniences.

The "inconveniences" DON'T have to be massive, by the way. Let's use the television example again. You don't have to sacrifice all of your television-watching in order to achieve your goals.

If you have a few favorite shows, by all means watch them! Recharging your mental and physical batteries with some downtime is just as important as working efficiently on your goals.

Again, the important thing is **balance**. Be willing to sacrifice what you don't need for something you really want. Rather than focusing on what you're giving up, focus on what you are gaining in the long run.

See success as something you need to incorporate into your life. If your life is already crammed full of unproductive activities and unsuccessful outcomes, you need to do a little housecleaning before success can effectively squeeze through your door.

(Note: cleaning up your physical surroundings can also be effective in helping you let go of unproductive activities! Clutter (mental or physical) is a horrible drain on your energy. Get rid of what no longer serves you and you'll be amazed at how much lighter and motivated you feel).

> I've been polite and I've always shown up. *Somebody asked me if I had any advice for young people entering the business. I said:* "Yeah, show up.
>
> **– Tom T. Hall.**

Conquering the Fear of Success

While the fear of failure is a clear reason why many of us avoid pursuing our goals, there is another fear that is often harder to recognize: the fear of success.

Why would you be afraid of success, you ask? There are several reasons:

- **Lack of belief in yourself.** If you don't truly believe in your own ability to get (and stay) successful, you will avoid forward progress at all costs. You may subconsciously feel that even if others believed you to be successful, you would still feel like a fraud. That would be an uncomfortable position to be in, so you hold yourself back until you feel "ready" to be successful.

- **Fearing increased responsibility.** You might be resisting a higher level of achievement because you don't feel capable of handling all the responsibility that would inevitably come with it. Once you become successful, you will have certain obligations and steps that need to be taken in order to maintain your level of success. That can be frightening and intimidating, and you may doubt your ability to handle new challenges you will face.

- **Low self-worth.** If you don't believe you deserve to be successful and happy, you will naturally gravitate toward a position in life that matches your self-image. If you believe you deserve to be earning $15,000 per year, you will continue to do so. Trying to force yourself to increase your income will be futile because subconsciously you will resist it. You will view increased abundance with suspicion, wondering "what's the catch?" – even if there is none!

- **Worries about what others will think**. This actually goes along with low self-worth. You may have a habit of letting others define you rather than forging your own path. You might believe that rich and successful people are dishonest, cruel, rude, cold, greedy, or any number of other stereotypes.
- **General negative expectations**. You may not have any identifiable fears about success, but rather experience a general sense of uneasiness or resistance to it. You might simply be afraid of the unknown, or pessimistic about the longevity of your success.

There are many more possible reasons to fear success, but they don't matter for the purposes of this book. What does matter is figuring out what YOUR fears are (if you feel you may have some).

Here is a simple exercise to help you know for sure if you might be afraid of success:

Give some thought to what success means to you. What vision do you have for your life? What can you see yourself doing, how much money can you see yourself earning, where can you see yourself living, etc.? Write this information down.

Now read it again. If you were able to step into this new reality right now, how would you feel? Would you hesitate? Maybe tell yourself that it's too good to be true? Would you shy away from one part of your vision or another?

Take your time and think about this for as long as you need to, because your fears WILL make themselves known if you give them the opportunity. Once they do, you will be able to work through and resolve them forever.

Hint: most fears relating to success are completely groundless. We fear the possibility of something happening, but such an occurrence is so remote that it's not even worth worrying about. Ninety-nine percent of the time, we realize we were just being paranoid.

However, even with realistic fears that aren't so groundless, we are usually pleased and surprised to discover that we already have the ability to work through any challenges they may present.

The realization of our fear ends up not being such a big deal after all.

If, during the above exercise, you can't come up with a single uneasy feeling regarding your success, then it is possible that you simply don't have any fear of success. Not everyone does. Your sole obstacle might be staying disciplined, or forming a solid plan, or even simply getting clear about what you really want.

Goal-Setting, Simplified

Goal-setting is one of those things that seems like it should be very simple, but can often cause anguish and aggravation. Even worse, if it's not done productively it can convince us that we're doomed to failure and prompt us to give up on our dreams forever.

The number one mistake that most people make when goal-setting is reaching too high right from the get-go. There is nothing wrong with reaching high – in fact I encourage it. However, what most people fail to consider is the PROCESS of growth and development that must take place between where they begin and where they'd like to end up.

You wouldn't expect an infant to set a goal to climb Mt. Everest, would you? Perhaps later when that infant has learned how to crawl and walk, and after he has grown into a man and strengthened his body and conditioned himself to deal with the harsh elements, and after he has tackled smaller and less dangerous mountains – yes. But not before the necessary growth, development and preparation have taken place.

Many people try to make a similar large leap when they set their goals. They want to transform themselves from a position of lack and fear to a position of power and success in a short period of time, and it's just not likely. (Notice I didn't say it was impossible!

Stranger things have happened, but let's just say it's a rarity.)

The good news is that every large goal can be broken down into smaller, more manageable goals. If your goal is to climb Mt. Everest, you will first need to gain some experience mountain climbing, get into the best shape of your life, and so on. (I will assume that you are not an infant, so you have already mastered crawling, walking, and growing into an adult).

Now, take another look at those smaller goals I listed above: gain mountain- climbing experience and get into great shape.

Even those steps can be broken down into smaller goals, such as buying some books or taking some classes to educate yourself on hiking and mountain climbing; joining a gym, starting a healthy eating plan, etc.

Successful goal-setting is as easy as learning how to identify the mini-goals that compose each larger goal, and focusing your efforts on THOSE FIRST. That doesn't mean you can't keep your larger goal in mind and keep pushing yourself to reach it. However, giving most of your attention to the smaller steps along the journey will result in less stress and much quicker progress.

Take another look at the vision you wrote for your life, and then ask yourself how this big achievement might be broken down into smaller steps. If you can come up with some reasonable action steps you can take immediately, you will gain confidence with each small achievement you make. As your confidence grows and you gain experience and knowledge, your action steps will automatically become bigger and bolder, and so will your results.

While you may be tempted to set a timeframe for accomplishing your goals, I would advise caution. It's okay to have an idea about when you will reach your goals because it can definitely keep you motivated and focused. But it can also backfire if you don't see results quickly enough and make you give up out of sheer impatience.

What I said in the segment about expectations also applies here. Be reasonable and balanced about your goals. Just like you can't expect to make a giant leap from "here" to "there", you also can't expect to accomplish everything overnight.

There are two good ways to keep your goal- setting balanced:

- Focus on the sense of accomplishment you get from every step you take. Rather than pinning your satisfaction only on the big goal you have in mind, allow yourself to feel good about the progress you're making toward that goal. Feel proud about the great job you're doing and really allow yourself to enjoy the journey.

- Don't worry about the timeframe. This one is definitely more challenging, but it's also very freeing! Instead of setting a timeframe, simply commit to working steadily and enthusiastically on each small action step. Don't buy into impatience if you don't see results immediately – in fact, let the ACTIONS themselves be their own rewards. Feel good that you are strengthening your self-discipline and growing more completely into the person you were meant to be. Believe it or not, it's very rewarding to take this type of attitude.

Again, do what you feel is best for YOU.

Taking Action: Like a Match to Tinder

Remember in a previous chapter I said that your attitude is like the yeast added to your bread recipe? ACTION is like the heat from the oven that merges all the ingredients and transforms them into a delicious treat.

Without action, everything I've said in this book so far is worthless. Perhaps "worthless" is too strong a word. There is merit in developing a mind-set of success, in adopting a positive attitude, and in learning to love yourself. These habits can continue to serve you in positive ways even when you're not working toward a goal.

As important as that is, action is undoubtedly a crucial aspect of success. You can set goals and change your mind- set until you are blue in the face but if you never take action, nothing will change in your physical surroundings.

> The people who get on in this world are the people who get up and look for the circumstances they want, and, if they can't find them, make them.
>
> – George Bernard Shaw

How to End Procrastination

Many of us fear taking action. We love making lists, forming plans and learning new techniques but when it comes to putting it all into motion, we freeze. We procrastinate. We hesitate. We find excuses not to work on our goals anymore.

Or, we do take action, but not on the important stuff. Oh no, we do more research, we refine our plans, we keep ourselves very busy so it SEEMS like we're taking action – but we're actually just killing time.

The most common reason for this fear (besides the ones we've covered so far: fear of success, low self-worth, worries about what others will think, etc.) may surprise you: fear of commitment.

We are afraid that once we begin moving forward we will be officially locked into our goal and we are suddenly forced to sink or swim! If we can simply avoid taking action, we can remain safely in the planning stage and not risk anything. We can convince ourselves that we did all we could, but it just didn't work out, there were circumstances beyond our control - so it's not OUR FAULT that we're not successful.

There is also another possibility, another reason why taking action seems so hard: sheer intimidation. This fear is often greatly reduced by setting reasonable goals, but we can also be irrationally fearful about moving forward even if our goals seem manageable.

The most effective way to deal with a fear of taking action is to simply disregard it and take action anyway!

That sounds like an impossible challenge if you are feeling paralyzed by fear, but I do have a bit of advice that should make you feel better. The fear of taking action almost ALWAYS vanishes shortly after you begin moving forward. You suddenly realize that you were worrying over nothing, and you actually begin to enjoy making progress. If you keep with it long enough and frequently enough, exhilaration takes over and you find you can't hold yourself back any longer. What a wonderful feeling that is!

If you absolutely feel terrified about taking action, take some time to look over your plans and come up with one SMALL action step that you can take immediately. Just one! Then take it. Then pick another small action step, and take that one too.

Making Your Action Steps Focused

However – make sure your action steps are FOCUSED. Taking random action can be a good start sometimes (if nothing else, it can help build your confidence), but ultimately you'll be going in circles.

Instead, take a few minutes to identify the key steps that will create RESULTS. Think about the actions that will attract opportunities, get the attention of those in a position to help you, and create steady progress.

Then keep up with this process, gradually increasing the size or magnitude of your steps. If you don't see immediate results, don't despair! Keep at it and in a very short period of time you should be feeling much more confident and eager to keep going.

Staying Motivated

Most of us have no problem feeling motivated when we first set our goals, but that inner fire dies pretty quickly sometimes. It might be due to an intimidating obstacle that appears in our path, or a sense of impatience when we don't see results as quickly as we'd like.

How do you regain your motivation when you run out of steam, and can you do anything to KEEP yourself feeling motivated? Yes!

Remember that motivation is a state of mind, just like discouragement. And like all mind-sets, you can choose which one you want to focus on.

Here are some great tips for staying motivated, even if you're not yet seeing the results you want.

Remember Your Dream

If you haven't already, write a detailed description of your ultimate dream. Take your time with this and avoid editing yourself! Just call up a mental vision of your dream and consider how it will change your life for the better. Write down as many details as you can. What type of person will you be? How much money will you have? What will your home look like? What will your relationships be like? How will you FEEL on a daily basis?

Write it all down in present tense (as if it were your reality today) – and read it to yourself every single day.

When we are confronted by fear and frustration, it's easy to forget what we're fighting for. It's easy to let the importance of our dream dwindle away, and hope that maybe "someday" we'll have the determination to make it happen.

Don't let your dream die! Keep it sharp and clear in your own mind. Honor it and vow to keep moving toward it, no matter what it takes.

Reinforce the Benefits

If you find yourself losing steam and feeling overwhelmed by obstacles, take a sheet of paper and write down the benefits of your dream using the detailed description referenced above.

On this new sheet of paper, make a list of the BENEFITS of your dream. A "benefit" is something you stand to GAIN.

So, for example, if part of your dream description goes something like this, "I am happily working for myself, doing work I love, and earning $100,000 per year" – then add these words to your list of benefits:

- Happiness
- Freedom
- Abundance
- Passion
- Fulfillment

Keep going until you have a long list of everything you stand to GAIN by continuing to work toward your goals.

After reading through this list and comparing it to how you feel right now, you should be more determined than ever to keep working toward your goals because acceptance of anything less is unthinkable.

See Obstacles as Mere Detours

One of the most common reasons we lose our motivation is because we feel overwhelmed or intimidated by unexpected obstacles. We can have the strongest motivation in the world, and suddenly one little thing will throw our plans off-course, and we freeze. Or worse, we view obstacles as "signs" from the universe that we're not "meant to succeed."

Rather than allowing this to happen to you, simply CHOOSE not to let it bother you. Say to yourself, "An obstacle is nothing more than a detour on my path. I'll find a way around it because I'm NOT giving up!" Just thinking a thought like that can empower you to begin moving forward again, even if you were initially intimidated.

Hint: a funny thing about obstacles is that they are usually as daunting as we CHOOSE TO MAKE THEM, according to our expectations. If we moan and groan and fall to the ground in hysteria, the obstacle seems to grow bigger and more intimidating. If we instead shrug our shoulders, roll up our sleeves and don our battle gear – the obstacle shrinks to the size of an anthill, and we can sidestep it gracefully.

> *Sometimes success is due*
> *less to ability than to zeal.*
>
> *– Charles Buxton*

Affirm the Possibilities

Another way we might lose our motivation is by beginning to doubt that our dreams are possible. When we first set our goals, we are convinced we can do it. But if results don't show up right away, we might start to doubt ourselves, or doubt that our dreams are "realistic" enough. After all, if it was meant to be, if we were meant to be successful, it would happen quickly and easily, right? Logically we might know that's pure hogwash, but emotionally we might feel like the universe is picking on us.

If you feel your conviction begin to dwindle, blast the doubt right out of your head by reading success stories of others who have accomplished the impossible. Seek out written stories or television programs about people who have overcome immense personal challenges to achieve success, and affirm that if they did it, you can too.

Better yet, WRITE YOUR OWN SUCCESS STORY! It might start out as fiction but you have the power to make it a true account. Here's a good opener for your story:

"___ (your name) never believed he (or she) had what it took to be successful, but that all changed when he decided to begin believing in himself. He decided to stop listening to the limiting beliefs that others tried to instill in him, and he made it his mission to rise above doubt and fear. With an iron determination, he went on to accomplish what others believed was impossible."

Make your success story as long as you like, and customize it to your unique situation. Read it whenever you need an emotional boost.

Avoid Burnout

Sometimes we get SO motivated that we might take on too much, too fast and end up feeling burned out. You'll know when this happens to you, because you start feeling stressed and overwhelmed, and irritated by even the littlest kinks in your plans.

You start feeling annoyed about having to work on your goals, and decide you'd

rather take a nap. HONOR that feeling. Go with it. Climb into bed and have a good rest. Go see a funny movie with a friend, or curl up with a good book by yourself. Go dancing, or sign up for some pottery classes or painting classes.

Do something completely unrelated to your goals, and **feel good about it**. We all need rest, recreation, and a reminder that there is more to life than pursuing our goals.

Enjoying the Journey

If there is one thing I want you to take away from this book, it is the understanding that success is a journey, not a destination. It's about what you do, but WHO you become through the achievement of your dreams.

Success is a process of letting go of perceived limitations, growing and developing as unique individuals, believing in our true potential, honoring the best parts of ourselves and sharing them with the world.

As we've learned throughout this book, most of this process takes place in our very own minds. We've always had the potential to be successful, we just needed to believe it and embrace it.

How freeing it is to realize that!

There are just a couple more points I want to expand upon, because I think they're very important.

Develop a True Attitude of Gratitude

I can't stress enough how crucial it is to have an attitude of gratitude. And not just in relation to your goals, either!

Gratitude can transform any aspect of your life, and most especially your thoughts. When you feel grateful for the good things in your life, you are obviously focusing more on them. This not only helps you to feel more positive on a regular basis, it also helps you to worry less about the negative stuff, lack, and struggle.

You feel happier overall, and everything in your life tends to run more smoothly. You feel optimistic, blessed, and grateful for the opportunity to mold your life into a work of art. Consequently, it becomes one!

Beginning today, make it a habit to express a feeling of gratitude for all the wonderful aspects of your life. At first you may struggle to find things to be grateful for. You may be so used to looking at the negatives that you truly can't see the positives! If you have to, start with the most obvious:

"I'm grateful for my healthy body, my ability to see and hear, the love of my family and friends."

With a little practice, you'll begin noticing more and more things to feel grateful for.

Express Appreciation for Everything

Appreciation seems similar to gratitude, but there are notable differences. Gratitude is usually a feeling of thankfulness for something you have, while appreciation is the practice of affirming or admiring the positive features of something.

For example: you can be thankful for the presence of someone you love in your life, and you can also appreciate the ways this person supports and encourages you.

Another example: you can appreciate the beauty of a morning sunrise, and you can also be thankful that it lifted your spirits and filled you with feelings of hope and inspiration.

Getting into the habit of expressing appreciation for everything in your life can keep you focused on the positive, just like an attitude of gratitude does. But it also makes the journey to success seem meaningful and worthwhile.

Take time to appreciate:

- Everything you have, for the joy they bring to your life.

- Everything you see or hear, for the ways they keep you focused in the present moment.

- The challenges you face, for the richness and strength they add to your character.

- Your journey itself, for the amazing experiences and growth it provides.

- Yourself, for your unique gifts, your indomitable spirit, your willingness to go the extra mile.

It's All Up to You

Your journey to success can be as simple and easy - or as difficult and painful - as you make it. Why not have fun with it?

Just as you convinced yourself that you were unlucky, unsuccessful and destined for failure, you can convince yourself that all of your dreams are right at your fingertips. By improving the quality of your thoughts, questioning your beliefs and daring to be bolder in your actions, you can achieve anything you desire.

Simply open your mind to the possibilities and be willing to give yourself a chance.

Learn how to relax and enjoy yourself.

Don't worry so much. Be willing to make mistakes, or take a scenic detour from the path before you.

Trust yourself and trust the universe. Open your arms and welcome in the abundance and joy waiting for you.

Don't grasp at it in fear, but instead let it flow gently and naturally. And it will.

> *'To live only for some future goal is shallow. It's the sides of the mountain that sustain life, not the top.'*
>
> *– Robert M. Pirsig*

The Deepest Desire of Your Heart

By Will Edwards

Find and Fulfil Your Unique Purpose in Life

Using the exact methods taught in our program, very many people are already producing amazing results in their lives; and so can you.

Our outstanding program represents the culmination of many years of research into the application of the principles of success; and everything you need to accomplish the most amazing transformation of your life is included.

Discover Your Unique Calling

Stay On-Track to Achieve Your Mission Overcoming Obstacles

Getting from Theory to Making it Happen Professional Tips and Exercises

Identify Your Most Important Activities Complete System to Optimize Time How to Ensure You Achieve Your Goals

Let' Connect to talk more about your own desires and map out your success journey. On my website is a link to schedule a Free Discovery session www.drstemmie.com

Bonus Affirmations

Affirmations to Shift Your Mindset

1. "I am embracing change and growth in my life."

   Welcome new experiences and opportunities for personal development.

2. "I am in control of my own destiny and the direction I choose."

   Take charge of your path and make conscious decisions to shape your future.

3. "I trust in the process of transformation and growth."

   Believe in your ability to evolve and adapt, even through difficult times.

4. "I am open to new ideas and perspectives."

   Expand your horizons and be receptive to fresh insights and viewpoints.

5. "I release all fear and resistance to change."

   Let go of any apprehensions and embrace the potential for growth that change brings.

6. "I am constantly evolving and becoming a better version of myself."

7. "I am flexible and adaptable in the face of change."

   Develop resilience and the ability to adjust to new situations with ease.

8. "I welcome new opportunities with open arms."

    Be receptive to new experiences and possibilities for growth and success.

9. "I trust that every change in my life is for my highest good."

    Believe that the universe is guiding you towards the best possible outcomes.

10. "I am confident in my ability to navigate any challenges that arise."

    Face obstacles head-on, knowing that you have the strength and determination to overcome them.

11. "I am willing to step out of my comfort zone to grow and learn."

    Embrace the unfamiliar and recognize the potential for growth in new experiences.

12. "I release old patterns and habits that no longer serve me."

    Let go of behaviors and thought patterns that hold you back from reaching your full potential.

13. "I am committed to creating a fulfilling and purposeful life."

    Stay focused on your goals and values, and prioritize living a life that aligns with them.

14. "I am ready and willing to embrace the next chapter of my life."

    Look forward to new experiences and opportunities with excitement and anticipation.

15. "I trust my intuition to guide me through times of change."

    Rely on your inner wisdom to navigate the shifting landscape of life.

16. "I am capable of transforming challenges into opportunities."

    Turn obstacles into chances for growth and learning.

17. "I am grateful for the lessons and growth that come with change."

    Appreciate the value of personal development and the experiences that facilitate it.

18. "I am at peace with the natural ebb and flow of life."

    Accept the inevitability of change and adapt with grace and ease.

19. "I am courageous and resilient in the face of change."

    Face new situations with bravery and the determination to persevere.

20. "I embrace my personal evolution with love and acceptance."

    Celebrate the journey of self-discovery and personal growth with compassion and understanding.

21. "I am open to receiving guidance and support during times of change."

    Welcome assistance and insight from others as you navigate new experiences.

22. "I am committed to staying true to myself amidst change."

    Maintain your authenticity and integrity as you adapt to new situations.

23. "I am a powerful creator of my own reality."

    Believe in your ability to manifest the life you desire through conscious choices.

24. "I trust that my life is unfolding in perfect timing."

    Have faith in the timing of events and the natural progression of your life.

25. "I am willing to release anything that no longer serves me."

    Let go of relationships, habits, and beliefs that hinder your growth and happiness.

26. "I am ready to embrace new beginnings and fresh starts."

    Welcome the opportunity to start anew and create a fulfilling life.

27. "I am grounded and centered, even during times of change."

    Maintain inner stability and balance as you navigate life's transitions.

28. "I celebrate my growth and the positive changes I've made."

    Acknowledge and take pride in the progress you've made in your personal development journey.

29. "I am adaptable and resourceful in any situation."

    Develop the ability to find creative solutions and adjust to new circumstances with ease.

30. "I am open to the wisdom and guidance of the universe."

    Trust in the support and guidance from the universe as you navigate life's changes.

31. "I find strength and courage within myself during times of change."

    Believe in your inner resilience and ability to face challenges head-on.

32. "I am committed to continuous growth and self-improvement."

    Dedicate yourself to lifelong learning and personal development.

33. "I trust that I am on the right path, even when it's uncertain."

    Have faith in your journey and the direction you're heading, even during times of doubt.

34. "I welcome change as an opportunity to grow and learn."

    Embrace new experiences and the potential they hold for personal growth.

35. "I am surrounded by love and support during times of change."

    Recognize the presence of those who care for you and are there to support you through transitions.

36. "I am in alignment with my highest purpose and potential."

    Strive to live a life that is in harmony with your true self and goals.

37. "I have the power to create positive change in my life."

    Believe in your ability to make a difference in your own life and the world around you.

38. "I am willing to let go of old stories and limitations."

    Release any self-imposed constraints or beliefs that prevent you from reaching your full potential.

39. "I am confident in my ability to thrive in any situation."

    Trust in your capacity to succeed and flourish, regardless of the circumstances.

40. "I am open to new experiences and the growth they bring."

    Welcome the opportunity to explore new situations and the potential for personal expansion.

41. "I am grateful for the journey and the lessons learned along the way."

    Appreciate the value of your life experiences and the wisdom they provide.

42. "I am fearless in the pursuit of my dreams and passions."

    Chase your aspirations with courage and determination, undeterred by obstacles or setbacks.

43. "I am in harmony with the natural flow of life."

    Find balance and inner peace by aligning yourself with the rhythm of the universe.

44. "I embrace the uncertainty of change, knowing it leads to growth."

    Accept the unknown with open arms, understanding that it is a catalyst for personal development.

45. "I am constantly evolving, shedding old layers and becoming my best self."

    Acknowledge and celebrate the ongoing process of personal transformation.

46. "I am capable of making positive changes in my life and the lives of others."

    Believe in your ability to make a difference and create lasting, meaningful impact.

47. "I am committed to living a life of purpose and intention."

    Focus on creating a life that is guided by your values and aspirations.

48. "I trust my inner wisdom to guide me through life's transitions."

    Rely on your intuition and inner guidance to navigate through change with grace and ease.

49. "I am open to new possibilities and opportunities for growth."

    Stay receptive to new experiences and the chance to expand your horizons.

50. "I am a powerful force for positive change in my own life and the world around me."

Affirmations to Unlocking Your Path to success

Here are some success affirmations you can use to build on your success muscle.

If you like, you can write down the success affirmations and post them around the house, or you can always bookmark this page and use it as a reference throughout the day when you need to give yourself a little pep talk.

Just remember, you are successful in many ways, and a lot of those ways are different than everyone else's. When you recognize your successes, you recognize how great life really is.

Affirmations for Overcoming Fear

1. My fear does not define me. I acknowledge it and do the thing anyway.
2. I radiate courage and determination.
3. I am making a conscious decision to change my life for the better. I am ready to do what it takes.
4. **I am grateful for this fear, as it shows that I'm going in the right direction.**
5. I vibrate on a positive frequency that only allows good things with the same vibe into my life.
6. I have the power to create my life and choose its course. Even when it's scary, I'm behind the wheel and I'm going forward.
7. **I am filled with endless possibilities.**

8. I am excited to see the success that comes after I overcome my fears and do it!

Affirmations for Fear of Change

More often than not, all fears we experience come from one core fear we all have: fear of the unknown.

Our instincts tell us that staying in the same place in the same state and doing things in the same way we are used to is safe and familiar. And changing something means stepping outside of the comfort zone into the scary unknown zone. Naturally, our subconscious mind aims to prevent this from happening in any way possible, which leads to all kinds of self-sabotaging behaviors.

If we let these instincts win, we usually end up staying in our "safe" miserable state and in one way or another convince ourselves that it's a smart decision. At least for now…

Positive affirmations for fear of change help you reframe stepping into the unknown so it doesn't feel so dangerous and scary anymore. It focuses your vision on the positive side of the possible change and the benefits you are potentially getting by going there.

Basically, affirmations calm down your instincts so they don't shoot an automatic aggressive response to sabotage your happiness!

1. **I am in the process of positive change.**
2. I have the power to change every aspect of life I want for the better. Change is good.
3. I am not afraid of the unknown. It's gonna be a lot better than this comfy but miserable present.
4. **Change is a constant part of life. I accept it and welcome it.**
5. Change is always for the better, even if I don't see or understand it right now.
6. I am excited to live in my new better reality.
7. I can make it through this, just as I made it through everything else in the past.
8. Affirmations For Fear Of The Future
9. I'm gonna do my best today to secure a good future.
10. Every moment is a new future, and there is nothing scary about the next moment.
11. I am letting go of worrying about things I can't control.
12. **I made it to today; I'll make it to tomorrow.**
13. I'm not gonna waste any more time. I'm ready to live in the present and enjoy my life to the fullest.
14. I inhale courage, I exhale fear.
15. Future is coming inevitably, and it's going to be wonderful.

Best Affirmations for Fearlessness and Strength

1. I am strong. I am courageous. I am powerful.
2. I welcome challenges and face them with excitement.
3. I believe in my ability to do this.
4. I can conquer any goal I set for myself.
5. **I recognize fearlessness as one of my features and I use it to follow my dreams.**
6. I am grateful for every challenge that comes my way and teaches me something.
7. I am unstoppable!
8. Affirmations To Overcome Fear Of Failure
9. Failed ventures always make great stories.
10. There is no success without failure. Every successful person had failed many times, it's simply part of the process.
11. **I am doing the best I can, and it's better every time.**
12. Every failure makes me stronger. And smarter.
13. I am learning so much with each failed attempt that I am bound to succeed.
14. **I choose to be successful no matter what and the fear of failure can't stop me.**

15. I can only fail if I stop trying.
16. Affirmations For Fear Of Success
17. Success is amazing, and I believe I deserve it!
18. I am strong and courageous, I can do anything I put my mind to.
19. I am willing to be successful and accomplish all of my big dreams.
20. **I am capable of becoming successful. I can easily bear all the responsibilities that it entails.**
21. It is safe for me to go to the next level and be successful.
22. I am not alone. Many great people achieved this success, and I can too.
23. **People who truly love me will always support me on my journey.**
24. I am meant to be successful! Nothing can stop me from reaching my goals.
25. Affirmations For Anxiety And Fear
26. Life is good. It is meant for me to enjoy it.
27. I am strong enough to face and overcome this.
28. **With every breath I take, I inhale calmness, I exhale fear.**
29. I feel anxious now but it will go away. I will make it through as I always do.

30. I am in control. I have the power to manage my fears and emotions.

31. Whatever happens, I'll survive it and learn from it.

32. Everything is okay. I can breathe freely and trust the process.

33. Affirmations For Fear Of Rejection

34. It's okay to be rejected sometimes, it's not the end of the world.

35. **If I get rejected, I open my eyes wider and look for other opportunities.**

36. Random person's rejection doesn't affect me in any way.

37. If a door is closed in front of me, I know there is a better door opened for me somewhere.

38. I feel relaxed and confident in social situations.

39. **I am not defined by anyone's opinion.**

40. Each rejection is an opportunity for me to learn and grow.

41. Affirmations For Fear Of Being Judged

42. People are kind. And if they aren't, they aren't my people.

43. I am not affected by anyone's opinion. I know my worth.

44. People don't think about me as much as I would think.

45. **I am happy, positive, and immune to judgement and negativity.**

46. Some people are just cruel. If they say ugly things, it's all about their ugly personality and it has nothing to do with me.

47. I can express my creativity freely without being judged.

48. I am a badass!.

49. Affirmations To Overcome Fear Of Death

50. I can enjoy my life freely as I'm protected by a higher power.

51. **Death is a natural process but not interesting enough to think about. I'd rather focus on life!**

52. I feel gratitude that I get to wake up in the morning, and I'm determined to not waste this day.

53. I understand there is no logical reason to fear for my life.

54. I am living my life to the fullest, enjoying every day I am blessed with.

55. **I feel safe and protected wherever I go.**

56. I am mindful and deeply invested in the precious present moment.

57. Affirmations For Fear Of Intimacy

58. Creating an intimate close connection is easy and natural for me.

59. I am good enough as I am and worthy of all kinds of love.

60. **I am building a relationship in which I'm prepared to fully share my life with my partner.**

61. It's okay to let someone I love into my heart... and my bedroom.

62. I treat my partner with kindness and respect, and get the same in return.

63. **As I open my heart to my partner, I allow our relationship to grow stronger.**

64. Intimacy and openness take my relationships to the amazing next level.

65. Affirmations For Fear Of Abandonment

66. I am enough and worthy of loving relationships.

67. Good people I meet become my friends and stay in my life forever.

68. I am truly loved. Everyone is happy to have me in their lives.

69. **There is no reason to worry about losing my partner. We are amazing together and enjoy each other's company. I am focusing on what I have instead of fearing the future.**

70. I don't need to prove myself to anyone. I am good enough as I am.

71. I welcome long-lasting relationships and do my best to keep them strong.

72. Love doesn't need to be earned. Being genuinely loved is my natural birthright.

73. Affirmations For Paranoia
74. There is no reason to be afraid.
75. I am safe. I feel safe. I am protected. I feel protected.
76. People are kind and trustworthy unless they proved otherwise.
77. I pay attention to my surroundings and analyze everything with logic and a clear mind.
78. **I don't give my irrational fears the power to make decisions.**
79. I trust my intuition. My gut will always tell me if something is wrong.
80. I can always ask for help if I need it.
81. Affirmations For Fear Of Being Alone
82. It's okay and natural to be alone sometimes. There is nothing wrong with it.
83. **I am whole. I don't need anyone else to feel whole.**
84. I love spending time alone with myself. I enjoy quiet moments when I can hear my own thoughts and find time for self-care.
85. I treat myself with love and kindness and others treat me the same way.

86. I am at peace when I'm by myself. I have plenty of interesting activities on my list.

87. **I am never alone. There are wonderful people in my life I can reach out to whenever I feel lonely.**

88. I am love. I radiate love. I am open to love and meeting my soulmate.

Affirmations for Unlocking Your Path to Success

1. My success is my success. No one else has it.

2. Success lingers around me. I just have to grab onto it.

3. Where I focus my thoughts is where I will focus my efforts.

4. When I look at my past, I only see my accomplishments. I do not see failures.

5. Success isn't so much found on the day I get an award or receive a prize or promotion. It's found in the journey leading up to that day.

6. Success is a reality that I live in. No one is going to hand me success. Everything requires effort on my part.

7. Some things are harder to do than other things. Which ones do I want to do today?

8. My success is unlike anyone else's, and the more I share it with others, the more successful I will become.

9. Positivity leads to success in more ways than I will ever understand.

10. If I think it, I believe it. And if I believe in it, all I have to do is put in the work to make it real.

11. Success is found in so many other places in my life.
12. Take a look at my life and you will find success falling around me everywhere.
13. I have more things in my life I want to work on so that I can be successful in them.
14. I will not let the stress of yesterday burden me today.
15. Stress only burdens my success if I let it.
16. My life is all about balancing success and being humble.
17. I am thankful for the people I have watched become successful for they have been guides for my own success.
18. When I hear a negative comment today, I will identify it as such and then put a positive spin on it.
19. Success can be found in all areas of life and I will do my best today to make myself even more successful in each area.
20. Success and love go hand in hand. You can't have one without the other.
21. I will tackle several work tasks today that I have been putting off.
22. Success in the workplace is something to be proud of.
23. Today is the day I will try to get to know one of my coworkers better because good relationships in the office lead to more successful companies.

24. I am the director of success in my career.

25. In every direction I look, I see more prosperity.

26. Success starts with my believing in me.

27. When things are tough at home and in my life, I simply need to remind myself of my success and inner strength.

28. I can take care of myself and my own home and that in itself is something to consider a success.

29. My personal success is seen by others.

30. My personal success will always be an example for others to follow.

31. The only personal success I will ever experience is found within only me.

32. No one can experience my personal success because I truly am unique from everyone else.

33. Life has not handed me my personal success. I have worked for it.

34. I have all the skills I need to achieve my dreams and find the job of my dreams.

35. I am talented in many ways and personal happiness and success can be enjoyed through my talents.

36. Understanding my personal successes starts with understanding myself.

37. When I look inside myself, I remember how successful I already am.

38. I have the personal skills and abilities necessary to be a success in all that I do.

39. I will not listen to negative thoughts that cross my mind because they impact my personal success.

40. I am a successful parent who only gets more successful.

41. I am a success in the eyes of my children.

42. The way I parent my children impacts all areas of success in my life.

43. I have found success in many parts of my home life.

44. Showing my children how to be successful in all areas of life is the most loving thing I can do.

45. Getting back up after failures is the best way to show my children how to be successful.

46. I will not let yesterday impact the success I display to my children today.

47. My parenting success begins first thing every morning and never ends throughout the day.

48. I get the opportunity to show success every day in the eyes of my children.

49. My children watch success unfold before them every day through my actions.

50. I have a positive attitude that will bring me unlimited success.

51. My vitality, positive attitude, confidence, and self-belief are my greatest assets that will get me closer to a successful life.

52. I am completely prepared with everything I need to experience love, success, joy, peace, happiness, and abundance.

53. I am thankful for all of the abundance that flows constantly into my life.

54. I am grateful for all the abundance that finds its way to me daily.

55. Every day, miracles happen in my life.

56. I am strong enough to handle all the hurdles and challenges that cross my path.

57. To put me one step closer to success, I have bid farewell to old habits, and I am prepared to welcome new positive changes in my life.

58. Everything will work out for the good of all, today and every day.

59. As I move through my day, I appreciate all the good things that have come to me.

60. The things I do every day create constant prosperity, wealth, and abundance.

61. Wealth flows into my life constantly.

62. I have full faith in my ability to find whatever success I seek.

63. I am a winner, and every day, I conduct myself as a winner and do what it takes to find success.

64. I am surrounded by positive and supportive people who believe I can succeed.

65. I have all the tools I need to manifest my desires and make all of my dreams come true.

66. I am worthy of every good thing that life can offer me, and I am deserving of success.

67. I am focused on my success, and every day I pursue my vision and goals.

68. The universe has millions of opportunities, and I am ready to receive my share.

69. New ideas come to me endlessly, and these ideas help me find all of the success I deserve.

70. I am fully prepared right now for financial abundance, peace, and happiness.

71. I can experience success in all areas of my personal life if I will allow it.

72. I am a quick and excellent learner, and I have what it takes to learn what I need to know to make my dreams come true.

73. My strength allows me to power through challenges and end the day feeling productive and accomplished.

74. I become more accomplished, powerful, confident, and successful every day.

75. My mind is always open to new and exciting opportunities.

76. I am an organized person, and my organizational skills grow daily.

77. I naturally expect good things to happen to me because I have a positive outlook.

78. Every day, my business dreams are manifesting and moving me closer to success.

79. I use every challenge as an opportunity for improvement and growth.

80. As more abundance enters my life, more doors continue to open for me.

81. I remain calm in the face of challenges, and my calmness fuels my success.

82. I am constantly manifesting my business dreams.

83. I am a motivated person who works well under pressure.

84. I am enough just as I am, and I have all of the gifts I need to succeed.

85. I make wise decisions, and I have full confidence in the decision I make.

86. I have a lot to give, and I am contributing valuable things to the world every day.

87. I am fully aligned with the energy of abundance and wealth.
88. I am a wealthy person and will live the life of my dreams.
89. My positive attitude brings me continuous success in everything I do.
90. Success in the eyes of my children is what makes me truly successful.
91. I am a courageous person who makes positive changes in my attitude and my life.
92. My dreams of success are continuously manifesting.
93. I continuously climb higher without limits to my opportunities.
94. I am passionate about my work, which shows in everything I accomplish daily.
95. People look up to me because I am a positive person and an excellent role model.
96. I have released every block that ever held me back from finding prosperity.
97. I easily attract positive clients who recognize the value I bring to their lives.
98. I alone am the architect of my divine fate, and I am achieving the things I have dreamed about.
99. During times of personal struggles, it is my successes that pave the way toward victory.
100. I live every day in a constant state of abundance.

Believe in your potential to make a difference and create a better future for yourself and others.

The DrStem Empowerment Academy Women SelfCare Success

Training, Coaching, Certification

DrStem, President, & CEO of The Empowerment Academy, has been a trainer and coach for over 25 years. The Empowerment Academy's focus is to train, coach and certify women to start their own consulting/coaching, speaking and seminar businesses. Global women from such countries as USA, UK, Australia, German, Botswana, Zimbabwe, Mozambique, Jamaica, Bahamas, Barbados, Nigeria, South Africa, Mexico, India, Pakistan have attended her seminars, conferences, and coaching programs.

Topics Covered in individual/group certification, coaching, training and workshops include:

Group and Individual Coaching Programs

- Breaking Free from Limiting Beliefs- Unleashing Your Full Potential

- Unlocking Success: Unleashing the Power of Self-Love and Self- Belief

- Unlocking Your Financial Potential: The Money Magnet

- Unmasking Self-Sabotage: Unveiling Sneaky Ways We Undermine Success

- Unlocking Your Potential: Conquering Self-Sabotage

- Unleashing Your Authenticity: Overcoming the Imposter Syndrome

- Unleashing Your Full Potential: Conquering the Fear of Success

- Cracking the Code: Unveiling the Secrets of Men's Minds

- Rebuilding the Heart: Transforming Pain into Healing

- Unlocking Your Best Year: A Journey to Personal Transformation

- Reclaiming Your Power: Strategies to Stop Giving it Away.

- Transforming the Past, Empowering Your Future: Healing Your Life
- Declutter Your Life: Clearing Physical and Emotional Clutter
- Empowering Independence: Breaking the Chains of Codependency
- Reclaiming Your Inner Child: Nurturing and Healing Through Reparenting
- Rebuilding Trust: Learning to Trust Again
- Reclaiming Wholeness: A Journey to Rediscovering Your True Self

Workshops

- Breaking Free from Limiting Beliefs – Unleashing Your Full Potential Workshop
- Unlocking Success: Unleashing the Power of Self-Love and Self- Belief Workshop
- Unlocking Your Financial Potential: The Money Magnet Workshop
- Unmasking Self-Sabotage: Unveiling Sneaky Ways We Undermine Success Workshop
- Unlocking Your Potential: Conquering Self-Sabotage Workshop
- Unleashing Your Authenticity: Overcoming the Imposter Syndrome Workshop

- Unleashing Your Full Potential: Conquering the Fear of Success Workshop
- Cracking the Code: Unveiling the Secrets of Men's Minds Workshop
- Rebuilding the Heart: Transforming Pain into Healing Workshop
- Unlocking Your Best Year: A Journey to Personal Transformation Workshop
- Reclaiming Your Power: Strategies to Stop Giving it Away Workshop
- Transforming the Past, Empowering Your Future: A Workshop on Healing Your Life Workshop
- Declutter Your Life: Clearing Physical and Emotional Clutter Workshop
- Empowering Independence: Breaking the Chains of Codependency Workshop
- Reclaiming Your Inner Child: Nurturing and Healing Through Re-parenting Workshop
- Rebuilding Trust: A Workshop on Learning to Trust Again Workshop
- Reclaiming Wholeness: A Journey to Rediscovering Your True Self Workshop

Certification Programs

- EmpowerHer: Women's Issues Certification Program
- Radiant Woman: Empowerment and Wellness Certification Program
- EmpowerHer: Mastering the art of Speaking, Certification Program
- Empowered Entrepreneur: Women's Certification Program for Launching a Successful Business Certification Program
- The Self Love Coach Certification Program

If you are interested in learning more about these programs, coaching or about starting your own consulting business contact: DrStem at:

www.drstemmie.com or *www.bouncebackconference.com*

DID YOU ENJOY THIS BOOK?

If you enjoyed reading this book, you can help by suggesting it to someone else you think might like it, and **please leave a positive review** wherever you purchased it. This does a lot in helping others find the book. We thank you in advance for taking a few moments to do this.

THANK YOU

As a Free Gift to you, I added the following Audio Books to my YouTube Channel *(DrStem Be Encouraged)* for you to listen for FREE.

1. Beyond The Tears – Bruised But Not Broken
2. It's Time to Shift- From Fear to Faith Finding Your True Self
3. The Power of Prayer
4. Finding your true self

Notes

Notes